Indigenous Medicine and Health Care Among Paite Tribe of Manipur

About the Author

Nemthianngai Guite, a faculty in Department of Social Work, University of Delhi, earned her M.Phil. degree in Social Medicine from Jawaharlal Nehru University, New Delhi. Her Ph. D. work is on Indigenous Medicinal Substances and International Trade Treaties from the same university. Her professional interests cater to health catre and development, intellectual property rights and indigenous medicine, community health and social work, health issues concerning children, women and the indigenous communities.

She has published several research papers and articles in Journals of repute besides contributing towards social work related to HIV, AIDS and tribals through IGNOU as well as numerous professional bodies.

Indigenous Medicine and Health Care Among Paite Tribe of Manipur

Nemthianngai Guite

CONCEPT PUBLISHING COMPANY PVT. LTD.
NEW DELHI-110059

ISBN-13-978-81-8069-732-6

First Published 2011

Published and Printed by

Concept
Since 1974

Concept Publishing Company Pvt. Ltd.

Regd. Office:

A/15-16, Commercial Block, Mohan Garden
New Delhi-110059 (India)
Phones : 25351460, 25351794, *Fax* : 091-11-25357109
Email : publishing@conceptpub.com
Website: www.conceptpub.com

Editorial Office:

H-13, Bali Nagar, New Delhi-110 015, India

Cataloging in Publication Data--*Courtesy:* D.K. Agencies (P) Ltd. <docinfo@dkagencies.com>

Guite, Nemthianngai.

Indigenous medicine and health care among Paite tribe of Manipur / Nemthianngai Guite.

p. cm.

Includes bibliographical references (p.) and index.

ISBN 9788180697326

1. Paite (Asian people)--Medicine--India--Manipur. 2. Paite (Asian people)--Medical care--India--Manipur. I. Title.

DDC 610.95417 22

Foreword

It was a bright sunny winter morning a few December ago. I was basking in the sun, trying to catch up with the warmth of the sun missed in the preceding foggy and gloomy days. With my tea cup filled the third time, I was reading the draft proposal of the research on indigenous medicine, which finally shaped into a dissertation about a semester later. What impressed me then was the concern of the proposal writer for the unique characteristics of the population proposed for study. As the work progressed amidst discussions, and the dissertation took shape, clarity of concern unfolded. A good research was done to highlight the issues of indigenous medicinal system in a region which has been richly endowed with traditional knowledge base. I sincerely wished that it would not get clamped up in the documentation units and libraries. I hoped that it would transform itself into a book.

I was extremely pleased and got a sense of fulfilment when Thian, the then 'proposal writer' and the author of the present book, informed about the acceptance of the manuscript for publication. This again is a bright sunny winter morning, and in December, when I am reading the final production of a year long quest for knowledge on indigenous medicinal system! – And adhering to the request of writing the foreword!

This book, I would say, is a very timely contribution in the field of research on indigenous medicinal systems. Its worth enhances manifolds as it focuses on Manipur. Not much research has emerged for most of the Northeastern region, barring anthropological, ethnographic studies of the indigenous people. This book is of extreme relevance in the present context of international trade regimes focusing on patenting of indigenous medicinal substances.

Indigenous medicine, also known as traditional or folk medicine comprises medical knowledge system which developed over a period of time through generations within different societies and cultures. As far the historical records go, study of traditional medicinal substances can be traced back to about 5000 years. Ancient Sumerians, Egyptians and biblical literature have cited evidences. In India, health care givers like Charaka and Sushruta have practiced during the first millennium BC.

The present book has embarked upon understanding and highlighting the indigenous medicinal knowledge system and practices prevalent in the northeastern state of Manipur. In most South Asian countries up to 80 per cent population is dependent on traditional medicinal system for their primary health care needs. In the current growing demand for indigenous medicine and the international trade regime, this book further accentuates the need to address the issues related to the production, protection, and transmission of this knowledge on one hand, and feasible use and dissemination of its utility, on the other. The introductory chapter opens to initiate the reader into the international concern and response to indigenous medicine and the scenario in India, particularly in Manipur. Very convincingly she has articulated and suggested the need to consider the local issues in traditional medical system to strengthen the international medical systerm.

Indigenous medicine is transmitted orally from one generation to the other in the communities through specific members in specific families. This has been documented in the book. Indigenous knowledge often exists diffused in the communities and the families within. Some get the recognition as practitioners on the basis of their healing. For accepted credentials as a healer, it is important that a healer has strong beliefs; their healing is successful and matches with the beliefs of the community. Failure in terms of healing or use of a particular substance is likely to affect the reputation of the traditional knowledge of a practitioner. Generally there are those who use it almost always; those who resort to it in crisis, and those who believe in it selectively. The book cautions that the traditional beliefs in this regard are subject to tests for efficacy and safety.

Utilization of traditional medicine is pitted against the prevalent allopathic system. It is preferred as an alternative but not a first priority is well illustrated in the chapter on health, disease and care utilization. Accessing traditional medicinal substances for health care is not perceived as stationary. It is seen in context of other established systems and dynamic needs of the users. Adding to the plurality of the health care system, introduction of allopathic system of medical care gradually got accepted as an additional choice while seeking health care. However, the positions of the two systems—allopathic and indigenous, as dominant, have swapped their positions over time. Alongside social factors, physical factors assume immense importance in the given topographic relief of the state. Physical inaccessibility due to terrain and consequent poor infrastructure is a barrier in accessing care has been brilliantly documented. Other factors such as political and economic also exert pressure on the propensity to access care.

In the light of already over-burdened and under-funded public health care system, and the need to encourage local resources for promoting health recognized in the Alma Ata Declaration, scope of indigenous medicinal system has been very effectively affirmed. Locally available medicinal substances can be tapped and channelised for use at much lower cost, by evolving a system of procurement, distribution and utilization; and by training the local care-giving personnel both in the formal and informal system of health care utilization. Incorporation of local tribal medicinal substance as part of the ISM (Indian System of Medicines) being promoted in the country under PMGY (Pradhan Mantri Gram Yojana) since 2000-01 has been very appropriately suggested. The belief of the people in their local traditions is likely to accentuate preference for their local, familiar medicine than the one offered under system not so familiar to them. Thus, inclusion and promotion of local medicinal substances in ISM will build the faith of the physically marginalized populations in the policy-makers who often use the mainstream experiences and overlook the nuances of the local populations for most policy formulations. Inclusion will also reflect on the sensitivity of the policy-makers towards the local nuances of the northeastern states, particularly the rich traditions of medicinal knowledge. There is need to identify those systems, practices, therapies and drugs, which have proven efficacy and assured effectiveness. This can be achieved only when there is an understanding of the local systems which overlap with indigenous medicine; their strengths and weaknesses and the road map that will lead to the fulfilment of the health care needs of the people.

I congratulate the author for having penned down this book. Her present research on medicinal substances and international trade treaties, is also extremely relevant in the context of local resources utilization for enhancing health care, and minimizing health related distress. I sincerely hope that this will also enjoy a similar transformation into book.

Sanghmitra S. Acharya
Associate Professor
Centre of Social Medicine and Community Health
School of Social Sciences,
Jawaharlal Nehru University, New Delhi-1110067
India

Preface

The establishment of indigenous medicine programme as part of attaining primary health care at the World Health Organization in 1978 should be regarded as an important milestone in the resurgence of interest in indigenous medicine. In part, this resurgence of interest is also simply an acceptance of reality. The indigenous system of health care is low-cost, locally available treatments which according to WHO are utilized as source of primary health care by 80 per cent of the world's population in many developing countries. Government could hardly continue to ignore this reality. On the other hand, the priority for this government was to create a legal framework for standardizing and regulating diverse traditional medical practices within their borders.

Since independence, a number of changes have taken place, which had an impact on the lives of the tribal. These include the nature of development itself. Specific interventions through State agencies, which have had its effect on the livelihood, work, cultural practices, which include health seeking behaviour and this, have undergone change. Newer innovations and introduction of allopathic system of medicine have brought changes in the perception and practice not only in their various aspects of their life but also in their health seeking behaviour. They have started using the newer inventions since they have more choices when it comes to structures of provisioning in health. It is observed that the change in the larger socio-economic system is bound to produce changes in the subsystems.

The prevailing health and medical system, the western system, has unfortunately failed to meet the need of the world's majority. The failure of the Alma Ata Declaration in fulfilling its objectives of achieving Health for all by the year 2000 gives more urgency for looking at an approach that is alternative of the existing medical system. The government, which provided medicines free of cost to the PHCs, could not satisfy the growing demand for these drugs with its budget constraints and allocation to other aspects of health. Today there are no drug available in several PHCs set up by the government.

These are some of the issues that call for priority attention and perhaps a systematic study. The present book is a modest attempt in this direction. It seeks to understand the importance of indigenous medicine and people's belief system for sound health care. The study also explores the traditional concepts of health and healing. An attempt was also made to find a meaningful collaboration between indigenous and modern health systems. Thus, the focus of the study is to identify and examine the changes in health seeking behaviour of the people within the overall socio-economic milieu. Finally, it suggests ways and means to address issues and concerns towards promoting indigenous medicine for health care needs.

People living in tribal areas often face obstacles in accessing basic health care services due to remoteness and backwardness of the areas in which they live. Understanding the health care needs of tribal people in these difficult circumstances with special focus on utilization of tribal indigenous medicinal substances is significant for devising comprehensive programmes. Data on socio-economic status, knowledge on indigenous medicine, beliefs, practices, and health seeking behaviours were collected from traditional healers and service providers in the primary health centres in two villages — Mualnuam and Thuangtam in Churachandpur district of Manipur, India. The methods of data collection include survey, group discussions in-depth in tesvies and social mapping. The health care services as part of the larger public health domain, is in a very poor state both in terms of infrastructure and service providers. Nearly all the women respondents indicated their preference towards indigenous medicine or home made remedies and traditional healers at the primary stage of their illness. Thus, scope of indigenous medicine becomes important. People's belief in indigenous medicine can play a vital role in implementing Government programmes on improving and promoting Indian system of medicine in rural areas and at the same time recognizing the local tribal medicine.

I do hope that this book is going to help people engaged in the development and welfare of the indigenous communities in the creation of an enabling and encouraging atmosphere where indigenous communities would lead their life with self-sufficiency in primary health care needs or at least minimising illnesses and enhancing their quality of life in every sphere.

Nemthianngai Guite

Acknowledgements

The present work is the fruition of the constant support and encouragement of several people whose consistent faith and confidence helped me in completing the work. Mentioning all of them is nearly an impossible task. However a prominent few among them may well not be missed out.

I am extremely grateful to my supervisor, Dr. Sanghmitra Acharya for being so supportive and patient during all the stages of the implementation of the present work. Her depth of knowledge, suggesting books and library to refer, reading my work, spending her precious time with me in discussing and correcting, giving me valuable insights and her attention even to minor details have been instrumental in inculcating and developing a kind of research attitude in me. She always reposed faith in me and pushed for the completion of this work to a satisfactory head and on time.

Present work would have been difficult to complete without the help and cooperation of my respondents from both the villages. In spite of their preoccupation and, sometimes after a tiring day or ill health they spared their valuable time and freely discussed their opinions, beliefs and perception in regard to the questions asked. I earnestly thanked all of them. Cooperation of the Chief of both the villages, Thuangtam and Mualnuam in providing support and valuable information about the villages is also acknowledged.

Further I thanked my parents and other family members who have remained a source of constant encouragement and support without which it would have been impossible to pursue the work. They have enabled me to pursue my fieldwork to fulfil my research goals. In fact, their contribution can never be expressed fully in words. I am grateful to my mother and father for their help in gathering all the necessary Government documents and for their wholehearted support during my field study.

I must thank my husband Mr. Naveen Kumar Mahal for his love and support. I feel pleased and proud to have a life partner like him who has always encouraged and supported me, understood and empathized with my research constraints and achievements.

I express my thanks to Mr. Ashok Kumar Mittal, Managing Director and other staff members of the Concept Publishing Company Pvt. Ltd., New Delhi, for extending the much needed support for the publication of this work and for bringing out the work in print and for endowing it with rich production values. Indeed, this will go a long way in sharing my ideas with a wider audience.

Nemthianngai Guite

Contents

List of Tables, Maps and Figures

Tables

Maps

Figures

(4) Land Holding Pattern

Both the study villages have the same land holding pattern. Village land belongs to the Chief. Villagers can have houses and practice *jhum* cultivation on it. Chief with the help of his Councillors (Upa's) and village authority [illegible] every year certain portion of the land for *jhuming*. Chief, his councillors and village authority, just select *jhum* lands and then the general public follow suits through ticket system. Terrace cultivation at the foothills of the village is also done with the permission the Chief of the village.

(5) Housing pattern, assets and livestock

In Muallungthu village, 66.3 per cent of the respondents are living in *kutcha* houses (house with thatched roof, bamboo walls and floors), and 33.7 per cent are living in *pucca* houses (house with tin roof and wooden walls and floors). Electric power supply do not reach [illegible] [illegible] excluding others, mention [illegible] and two respondents [illegible] rice mills in the village [illegible] per cent of the [illegible] 20 per cent in [illegible] outside world. [illegible] both the villages, livestock [illegible] serve their daily [illegible] and as a goods carrier or [illegible] economic status of [illegible] enough [illegible] last for [illegible] the women play [illegible] animal husbandry, besides being [illegible]

1

Indigenous Medicine and Health Care

An Overview

Human life is inherently frail – from the inevitability of decay and death to that of disease and sickness. Alleviation of disease and preservation of health both conditioned by culture, have been a human pursuit since antiquity. Using drugs and diet as remedies for the disruptive episodes in life process, is not something new. It is as old as human existence. The pre-historic humans derived the therapeutic agents from nature without maligning the environment. The plant kingdom, since the beginning of human civilization, served as the reservoir of medicine – therapeutic agents to restore health. Overtime the need to cover a wider variety of disease patterns and to augment the therapeutic potential of the agents, mineral and animal constituents began to be incorporated into this plant based medicine. Needless to say, this used of natural resources as therapeutic agents was based on a unique belief system encompassing the concepts of health, physical or mental illness, diagnosis, treatment and of prevention. The accumulated knowledge of such health practices and products is a rich cultural heritage common to all human societies sometimes ignored or unrecognized in a formal or institutional sense.

INTERNATIONAL RESPONSE TO INDIGENOUS MEDICINE

In 1977, the Thirtieth World Health Assembly of the World Health

Organization (WHO) passed a resolution promoting development of training and research in traditional system of medicine. In the following year, in 1978, the International Conference on Primary Health Care held in Alma Ata under WHO and UNICEF sponsorship passed additional resolutions supporting the utilization of indigenous practitioners in government sponsored health care systems. This brought about the issue of improving and strengthening the public health infrastructure in all the signatories' countries including India.

As its declaration towards primary health care, WHO has taken up various activities and initiatives concerning indigenous medicine. In the progress report on indigenous medicine and modern health care presented by the Director General Dr. Nakajima at the 44th World Health Assembly in 1991, it was stated that WHO undertakes, in response to request from member states, are those that support member in their efforts to formulate national policies on indigenous medicine; to study the potential usefulness of indigenous medicine, including evaluation of practices and investigating of the safety and efficacy of remedies; to upgrade the knowledge and skills of traditional and modern health practices (Zhang, 1994).

At the international level, in 1988, the World Health Organization, the World Conservation Union, the World Wide Fund for Nature convened an international consultation on the conservation of medicinal plants in Chiang Mai, Thailand. This resulted, *inter alia*, in the issue of the Chiang Mai Declaration, calling for action to "save the plants that save lives" which helped in finalization of the guidelines on the Conservation of Medicinal Plants, published in 1993. Moreover, Resolution WHA41.19, taken at the Forty-first World Health Assembly (1988), drew attention to the Chiang Mai Declaration and endorsed the call for international cooperation and coordination to conserve medicinal plants, thereby placing their conservation firmly in the public health policy arena.

INDIGENOUS MEDICINE IN INDIA

In the case of India, our government has encouraged the traditional great medical systems such as Ayurveda, Unani, Siddha etc. However, a policy decision regarding the myriad culture-specific local medical systems is yet to be taken. India has perhaps the world's largest community supported living tradition of its own indigenous systems of medicine. Indian medical traditions function through two types of social streams, the folk stream and the classical stream. The folk medical stream is located in the villages of rural India; there is no tribal or rural community without a local health traditions, a system which is local resource based relying on locally available flora, fauna and minerals. So intense is the dependence on local resources that an ethno biological survey conducted by the All India Co-operative Research Project on Ethno Biology, covering 80 percent of the tribal areas, reported the use of 7500 wild plants for medicinal purposes by tribal groups alone. This amount to almost five percent of all the flowering plants in India (Mukhopadhaya, 1997). These medical traditions are generally undocumented and systematic attempts have not been made to evaluate their strengths and weaknesses. Who is competent enough to judge local health traditions and what methodology should be adopted to evaluate these traditions are questions, which have not been posed seriously. It is indeed remarkable that with over 10,00,000 practitioners as its carriers, the folk streams receives practically no state or organizational funding and is entirely supported by the community. Given its magnitude in terms of human power, natural resources and knowledge, folk traditions could be harnessed to achieve the goal of self—sufficiency in primary health care.

Scenario in North East India

The North East India, comprising the seven sister states, namely, Assam, Arunachal Pradesh, Nagaland, Manipur, Mizoram, Meghalaya, Tripura, have remained relatively backward even after fifty years of independence. The reasons for this backwardness or the lack of development are many. First, its location which is in the north east corner and joined to mainland India through a narrow corridor, hardly 80 kilometre wide. The rest of its land locked territorial boundary is shared by among Bangladesh, Myanmar, China and Bhutan, giving the North East a strategic position.

The ethnic composition of the North East is diverse comprising principally of Sino-Tibetan stock, who have migrated into India during different periods in history, mostly from Tibet and China through Myanmar and Thailand, and more recently after independence from Bangladesh. Migration from the plain areas of West Bengal, Bihar and Uttar Pradesh, though less significant is not totally absent.

The tribal population had been encouraged to pursue their tribal lifestyle and culture undisturbed following Nehru's Panch Sheel Policy. What he failed to recognize was the dynamics of tribal societies and the social changes that were taking place. This has been the source of discontent among the tribal people and has given rise to distinct political aspiration. Moreover, with low population densities the North East is poorly represented in the National Government (Hazra, 2002).

The real cause of the lack of development is the alienation of the North East and the failure to develop proper relationship between tribal and rest of India. Solving the problems of today's world requires a high degree of professionalism, openness and inter-disciplinary approach, the backwardness stemmed from geo-political realities. The planning and development did not take in consideration the real needs of the people. Lack of law and order has been blamed for the North East's underdevelopment. Technology has made little stride and foreign firms are reluctant to invest. Under such a situation it is required to evaluate the resources available and determine the needs of the people, so that a justified planning may be attempted.

Development and health are intricately related. The health status of the North East is perhaps related to backwardness and *vice versa*. Despite the stress on sanitation and preventive medicine in the pre-Independence period and the Bhore Committee recommendation of 1946, the post-Independence era has seen a virtual decline of preventive medicine and a major stress on curative medicine particularly in the North East India. Health planning has never been made an integral part of the overall planning for socio-economic development. Planners failed to realize the need to tackle unemployment, malnutrition, housing and sanitation problems along with the integrated health services for the entire population as the prime requisite for health attainment. But a number of vertical programmes like family planning programmes, etc., became the main focus of the health care system. Health education and public health were denied a priority and the budget allotted to health care never exceeded the 3 percent mark (Hazra, 2001).

The spatial health pattern of the North East shows both uniformity and diversity. Uniformity of pattern is seen in communicable diseases, which are strongly influenced by ecological factors, like acute diarrhoea, respiratory ailments, leprosy and malaria. These diseases are widespread throughout the area. Cultural parameters lead to diversities in health characteristics. This is portrayed in the incidence of cancers, and sexually transmitted diseases and AIDS. AIDS has secured a firm ground in Manipur, and to some extent in Nagaland. Cancer in Nagaland and Manipur is associated with the food and other cultural habits. The low population densities and the existence of alternative tribal or folk medicine compensate health care facilities though poor in the northeastern states of India. However, these tribal medicine needs protection and promotion on the part of the government; otherwise it may not compensate the health care services any longer. For the purpose of this study the state of Manipur is selected to explore the nature and utilization pattern of indigenous medicinal substances for primary health care needs. The State has about 6.20 percent of North East India's population (Census of India, 2001) but does not have a matching share of medical facilities available at the National level. Besides medical facilities are unevenly distributed, big hospitals, equipments for specialized treatment, specialist's etc. are all located in urban centres.

In North East India, the majority of the medicinal plant species (70 percent) occur in the forest areas and the remaining 30 percent are found in non-forest lands including lands under cultivation (Datta, 2001). The tribal people and the forest dwellers collect a variety of leaves, fruits, seeds, nuts, roots, barks, tubers and rhizomes which have medicinal value. However, marketing of medicinal plants faces serious problems. Trade in medicinal herbs suffers from market imperfections. Such imperfections are apparent both on supply side, and, on the demand side. Factors contributing to such market imperfections are: absence of a system of defining property rights; problems in arriving at a convincing patenting policy; unique characters of medicinal plants and uncertainty of their availability; knowledge of medicinal plants being restricted to a limited people; absence of organized market; interplay of middlemen etc.

UNDERSTANDING INDIGENOUS MEDICINE

What separates this body of knowledge referred to as 'indigenous medicine' from 'moder n medicine' is the fact that the latter in anchored in science, while the former is practical experience. As long as science continued to be narrowly defined, traditional medicine remained largely unnoticed (Mukhopadhya, 1992). It took a sort of scientific resolution, a paradigm shift, to draw renewed interest in traditional medicine. Increasingly the very validity of this traditional-moder n dichotomy is being questioned. Indigenous medicine differs from the 'moder n' or 'western' medicine not in terms of goals and effects, but in terms of their underlying cultures and historical contexts. Viewed from this perspective all medicines are modern in so far as it is satisfactorily directed towards the common goal of providing healthcare, despite the setting in time, place and culture (WHO, 1977).

Indigenous medicinal substances, their nature, axioms and practices varies from one country to another, or more precisely, from one culture to another. Even names, practices and products, vary from one place to another depending upon the socio-cultural heritage, religion and political identity. In India we have both the documented and non-documented form of traditional medicines. The Indian system of medicine recognized those originated in India as well as from other countries and got assimilated over the course of time. In this study the term 'indigenous medicinal substances' in use are synonymous with 'traditional medicine' for wider coverage. Its main focus is on non-documented/unofficial/unrecognized system of medicine, which is easily available and accessible to the people.

"Describing folk medicine as 'unofficial' health beliefs and practices, define it in contrast to 'official medicine' on the basis of authority. Something is official if it is authorized in a formal way. Folk health traditions are not given official standing by state agencies, and most lack formal authority structure of their own. There is no office among the folk herbalists in a region that can specify "standard procedure" or "regulate practice" (Hufford, 1997).

The term "indigenous medicine" or "indigenous systems of health care" refers to the long standing indigenous systems of health care found in the developing countries particularly among indigenous populations. The paradigms of these indigenous medical systems view humanity as being intimately linked with the wider dimensions of nature. The World Health Organization has referred to these systems as "holistic", i.e. "that of viewing man in his totality within a wide ecological spectrum, and of emphasizing the view that ill health of disease is brought about by an imbalance or disequilibria, of man in his total ecological system and not only by the causative agent and pathogenic evolution." The indigenous systems of health care are low cost, locally available treatments which according to WHO are utilized as source of primary health care by 80 percent of the world's population.

Emerging concern towards indigenous medicine

It is the feature of indigenous health systems that it intersects with areas of national economy than simply health. Environmental factors such as land degradation through erosion and/or development has contributed to the loss of natural habitats. Loss of natural habitats can affect the availability of medicinal plants and hence have an impact on local heath standards. In countries where this occurred, herb gatherers have to walk increasingly long distance to find herbs that previously grew nearby. Overtime medicinal plant resources deplete in those areas and the distance and time involved in gathering herbs increase. This is compounded in herbs where demand is great and cultivation is minimal. All this contributes to increasing cost, the availability and sustainability of naturally occurring sources of medicine (Bodekar, 1994).

Domestic finances as well as national economic development may be linked to the cultivation and use of indigenous medicine. For instance, cultivation and use of wild harvesting of medicinal plants can bring in additional source of family income. It also saves expenditure on other medicine. However, over harvesting constitutes a threat to biodiversity. Over harvesting of medicinal plants, as is the case of India, where approximately 80 percent of the raw materials for indigenous medicine and cosmetic products come from the wild sources, raise the need for new policies which integrate health and environment and economic perspectives. Investments are needs for the development of appropriate cultivation and harvesting strategies, which will meet the demand for low cost and locally available medicines as well as for the conservation of biological resources (Helly and Cherla, 1999).

In recent years, there has been a growing interest in indigenous medicine among the international pharmaceutical industry as well as among the natural product industry in Europe and North America. Indigenous medicine is viewed by the pharmaceutical industry as a source of 'qualified leads' in the identification of bioactive agents, which can be synthetically modelled for the production of patented modern drugs. These trends have led to a situation where indigenous medicinal substances are viewed as a source for the production of other medicine rather than having intrinsic validity and value of its own right. For instance in the case of malaria the synthetic drugs are no more useful as the mosquitoes have developed resistances against the drug. However, the original drug, i.e., the cinchona bark—the natural source of quinine, on which the synthetic drugs (chloroquine and mefloquin) are modelled and developed, is still effective in resisting malaria (Shankar and Venugopal, 2000).

Resurgence of interest towards indigenous medicine

In the past decades there has been a resurgence of interest and activities in indigenous medicine both in developing and developed countries. A number of factors contributed to this resurgence of interest. In brief, it may be cultural, economic, national crisis like war and epidemic to conserve biodiversity.

Cultural

The most important factor is the nationalist spirit that engulfed the developing countries on their independence from the colonial rule. With political independence from the colonizers, most of the developing countries experienced a sense of cultural revival. Reviving one's own culture and taking pride in it beçome a nationalist goal. This cultural revival renewed interest in traditional health practices and products among the indigenous people.

Economic

More recently, hard economic realities also contributed to this renewed interest in indigenous medicine. For many developing countries, the Western health care system became economically burdensome. This system, in most cases is based on institutions (hospital) with a curative focus. In many developing countries, hospitals are primarily located in large urban centres while the bulk of population lives in rural villages. These hospitals with their modern technology often consume more than 90 per cent of the health budget, leaving little resources for other essential activities. Drugs, produced by multinationals and often imported from outside are also a cost burden that few developing countries can afford. Faced with such economic pressure, government in many developing countries have recently increased their support for the long standing traditional medical practice for their primary heath care needs in tune with the WHO declaration.

National Crisis

It has served to spur developments to evaluate their indigenous medical traditions as a means of providing affordable and available health care for their citizens. Two common crises have been influential. They are war and epidemic (Bodekar, 1993). In the case of war an acute shortage of pharmaceutical supplies necessitate the country to turn to its herbal tradition as a means of assisting with the country's medical needs. For instance during the Vietnam war of independence, an official policy was articulated in 1954 by President Ho Chi Minh, which asserted the importance of preserving and developing indigenous medicine as a basic component of health care through out the country since modern medicine was not affordable for a significant proportion of the population of Vietnam. In the case of epidemic, example from Africa show that the government facing huge drug bills for the growing AIDS crises are looking to their indigenous medical traditions and medicinal substances to identify inexpensive and effective treatment for at least alleviating the suffering of AIDS victims. Also outbreak of chloroquine resistant malaria has also been a spur for a number of countries to re-examine traditional methods of treating malaria.

Conservation of biodiversity

International concern and pressure to conserve biodiversity is the latest source of influence on the promotion of indigenous medicine. Two other interrelated factors must also be noted: clinical tests on the efficacy of some indigenous medical practices (with positive outcome) and, consequently, a rush by some multinationals to patent and market those products. These latest development brought in various problems and issues.

HEALTH CARE SYSTEM AND STRUCTURE

Health care is just one of the inputs which determine the health of a given community. Health status is determined by a variety of socio-economic factors like income levels, education, nutrition, water supply, and sanitation. Therefore, WHO definition addresses health as 'a state of complete physical and mental well-being and not merely the absence of infirmity'. What is well recognized is that health care is not a mere technical input but is shaped by socio-political forces in the society. All societies have evolved means to alleviate pain and suffering caused by illnesses. Health care is at the very centre of concerns for an individual. Within the primary groups, for example the family, the individual forming the group mutually shares this concern for health. This mutual concern gets, in practice, translated into the responsibility that the head of the family, who manages the affairs of the household, bears for attainment and maintenance of the health of each individual member. The individual concern is, in other words transformed into a family responsibility. Individual and families derive their identities from the community in which they live. So, at the next stage, the community becomes the guardian of the health of its members. This role of the community in the sphere of health, as in several other aspects of community life, derives justification from the fact that most determinants of the health of its individual members lie embedded in the environment within and surrounding that community. The community is in a sense a social organization that mediates between its members and environment in order to sustain life and promote healthy living conditions within its geographical bounds. It has been widely recognized that environmental factors play a much more important role than the individual specific genetic factors in determining the conditions of health and mortality in a population. Therefore, it is one of the basic functions of social organization to cater to the health needs for its members (Bose and Desai, 1983).

Communities do not exist in isolation; they form part of a larger society, the nation or the state. Accordingly, a part of their concern for health gets transferred to this larger, more inclusive whole. The individual, the family, the community and the state can thus be seen as partners sharing unavoidable responsibility of ensuring that the opportunity of leading a healthy life is available to all, without discrimination of any kind (Bose and Desai, 1983).

In the provisions of health care, primacy attaches to the role of the individual, the family and the community. Apart from the above conceptualization, this proposition rests on the historical experience of indigenous cultures, which have persisted for long in most of the so called developing countries from the Middle East to the Far East. It is within such a cultural framework that an appropriate indigenous system of health and medical care had been evolved on no less a scientific basis than the one on which the edifice of 'modern' medicine has been built. Health care, thus, become an essential social service and the government provides free health care in government institutions.

As our proposed study is concerned with tribal societies, special attention was given to the utilization of indigenous medicine in dealing with health problems. Since independence a number of changes have taken place, which had an impact on the lives of the tribal. These include, the nature of development itself, specific interventions through state agencies, which had have its effect on the livelihood, work, cultural practices, which includes health seeking behaviour and these have undergone change. Newer innovations and introduction of allopathic system of medicine have brought change in the perception and practice not only in the various aspects of their life but also in their health culture. It is observed that the change in the larger socio-economic system is bound to produce changes in the subsystems. Banerjee in his work on health culture observed that health culture is the subculture of the larger complex of culture (Banerjee, 1982). As a result the changes in the overall culture influence changes in the health culture of the community. Therefore, a study that proposes to look at the utilization pattern of indigenous medicine has necessarily to locate it within the changes that have taken place with intervention specifically related to health as well as the larger socio-economic sphere. Also there is a need to understand how the changes in larger socio-economic sphere and the health care system have brought about the changes in the practice of folk practitioners.

System

The health care system of a society can be broadly defined as a set of ideas, practices and organizations, which have been developed to deal with problems of health and illness in the society. Numerous studies by medical anthropologists and sociologists in the past several decades have shown that the content of the health care system tends to vary from one society to another, depending upon social, historical and ecological circumstances (Lee, 1982).

Health systems comprise the whole array of elements or

components of the broader social system, which are related to the health, and physical, mental and social well-being of the population. While the medical systems or the health service systems comprise for the organized array of human resources, technologies and services specifically designed for the development and practice of a medicine for individual or collective health care. In a more strict sense, medical systems are made up of a more or less uniform set of schools, hospitals, clinics, professional associations and agencies that train personnel, maintain an infrastructure for biomedical research and deploy a network of services for varying degrees of complexity for the prevention, curing, care and rehabilitation of the sick (Pedersen and Baruffati, 1989).

Structure

Health care institutions have structural division for better performance of duties. It should have good facilities with skilled staff. But quite often we find that they face difficulty in running institutions because of changing health care needs; rapid advances in technology; obsolescence of equipment; rapid turn over of staff. Besides this problem there are other emerging problems in health sector. They can be stated briefly as –

- Dual diseases burden of communicable and non-communicable diseases;
- Technological advances which widen the spectrum of possible interventions;
- Increasing awareness and expectations of the population regarding health care services; and
- Escalating costs of health care and ever-widening gaps between what is possible and what the individual, institutions or the country can afford.

With these perspectives the study basically attempts to gather essential information needed for health planning. Health planning, in brief, needs to examine the following factors before implementing it. They can be –

- Current health status, health care needs and health care utilization pattern of the population;
- Available institutions/manpower/facilities;
- Quality assurance mechanism and cost of care data at primary, secondary, tertiary care levels;
- National and state level public goals; and
- Income and purchasing power of the people.

RATIONALE BEHIND SELECTING THE STUDY TRIBE

The study was undertaken to understand the utilization pattern of indigenous medicinal substances for health care needs in Manipur. It also tries to find out, if possible, a way for tackling the prevailing conditions characterizing the health scenario of Manipur. It is a multi-stage and purposive sampling. Manipur has nine districts, of which there are four plain districts and five hill districts. The hill districts are given more emphasis for the study because they constitute only the tribal population with no proper health facilities. Besides this, almost all the hill districts are overwhelmingly rural in character, few with the headquarters depicting a semi-urban nature. Out of the five hill districts, the district of Churachandpur was selected based on the area and size, population, sex ratio, literacy level, density of population etc. According to the census of Manipur 2001, Ukhrul, Tamenglong, Churachandpur, and Chandel are predominantly tribal districts having more than 90 per cent of the district's population as Scheduled Tribe (ST). Senapati district has recorded 78.5 per cent of its population as ST. These five districts together hold 92.4 per cent of the State's total ST population.

In Churachandpur district out of the many tribes, the 'Paite' tribe is selected due to the following reasons. Out of the many tribes residing in Churachandpur district, 'Paite' tribe holds the majority in terms of population and land occupation. As per the Census of Manipur, 2001, the total population of 'Paite' was 49,271 which is the highest among the other tribes residing within Churachandpur. In terms of educational level 'Paite' tribe has recorded the second highest literate population[1] and also recorded the highest in attending schools and any other educational institutions[2].

Based on this data, the Paite tribe is selected for the study as this tribe is advanced in many fields as compared to the other tribes residing in Churachandpur district and this seems to be the most appropriate tribe to represent other tribes in the district.

CONCEPTUAL FRAMEWORK

From early days man started living in equilibrium with nature. As man realized that he has to depend heavily on nature and natural resources for his daily requirement, he automatically developed curiosity and instinctive interest towards various plants and animals. This knowledge comprises their use not only for food and medicine but also for their basic needs. Such indigenous knowledge about plant, animals, agricultural practices and other aspects that affect the human being are of important strategic value and got wide ranging economic, social and political repercussions. Hence the need to protect and improve the traditional knowledge associated with the biological diversity arose and also came to be debated all over the country.

Looking from the sociological perspective we find that, through time indigenous medicine has sustained itself through processes deeply rooted in a society's socio-cultural complexes. 'Indigenous medicine is a set of concepts of health and illness that reflect certain values, traditions and beliefs based on the people's way of life, or culture. Indigenous medicine is just but one of the manifestations of the people's would view, how they relate and interact with themselves as individuals, as part of the community and rest of the environment' (Segesmundo, 1994). Probably or maybe here lies the secret of its sustainability and its relevance to people's lives even as it only primarily responds to people's health problems. There is wisdom in indigenous medicine that may help in developing health system that can be appropriate even at this time.

Therefore, for a health care system to be relevant to the people it serves, it must be suited to economic and socio-cultural conditions of the nation and fit in people's psyche or consciousness. Necessary, therefore, is a new conceptual framework that recognizes the interconnectedness of health with other aspect of the environment and that will lead to the development of a holistic approach and attitude towards health. This was laid down as the 'new holistic concept' of health by the World Health Organization in the late 1970s. Most developing nations realized that progress in the area of overall economic development is intricately related to the general health status of the population. They now understand that funds allocated for health programes do indeed constitute in economic terms not only a sound but also an essential investment. Further more, the need for services is as large in scope as it is urgent. Estimates indicate that 70 to 80 percent of the population of developing countries has little or no access to basic health services. At the same time the masses of rural inhabitants are becoming increasingly aware of what is achievable through modern medical care and governments are increasingly pressured to provide medical health services. However, these countries find it impossible to expand the health services network or even to improve the existing health services network using expensively staffed hospitals and health centres, as the world inflation mounts and the financial situation of countries with low production worsens. Given this scenario, the idea of effective low-cost health care delivery system was introduced, as it became inevitable and emerged as an obvious alternative.

The establishment of indigenous medicine programme as part of attaining primary health care at the World Health Organization in 1978 should be regarded as an important milestone in the resurgence of interest in indigenous medicine. In part this resurgence of interest is also simply an acceptance of reality. The indigenous system of health care is low-cost, locally available treatments which according to WHO are utilized as source of primary health care by 80 percent of the world's population in many developing countries. Government could hardly continue to ignore this reality. On the other hand, the priority for this government was to create a legal framework for standardizing and regulating diverse traditional medical practices within their borders.

International concern and pressure to conserve biodiversity is the latest source of influence on the promotion of indigenous medicine. Two other interrelated factors must also be noted: clinical tests on the efficacy of some indigenous medical practices (with positive outcome) and consequently, a rush by some multinationals to patent and market those products. These latest developments brought forth a plethora of problems and issues, but at the same time ushered in a new era for indigenous medicine. This contemporary focus on indigenous medicine has also brought forward other related issues. These issues may be grouped under four broad categories:

- Preserving and promoting indigenous practices and products;
- Collaboration/cooperation of indigenous and modern systems of health care;
- Production/research and development of indigenous medicine with full attention to all the complex issues of intellectual property rights, patent rights, the role of multinationals, etc.; and
- National and international policies regarding indigenous medicine and biodiversity, and environmentally and culturally sustainable and equitable development.

These issues are complex and critical. Most of them transcend national boundaries and cannot be resolved without international efforts and agreements. It is time that we embark on a serious dialogue, both within and among nations, to address these fundamental issues for human health in all its dimensions. With this conceptual framework in mind, the research study is carried out in quest for better understanding of the importance of indigenous medicine and people's belief system for sound health care by drawing on the traditional concepts of health and healing as well as locally available modern facilities and also to find a more meaningful collaboration between indigenous and modern health systems.

OBJECTIVES OF THE STUDY

The present research was carried out to understand the importance of indigenous medicine and people's belief system for sound health care. The study also explores the traditional concepts of health and healing. An attempt was also made to find a meaningful collaboration between indigenous and modern health systems. Thus, the focus of the study was to identify and examine the changes in health seeking behaviour of the people within the overall socio-economic milieu. The following are the specific objectives –

- To examine the utilization pattern of indigenous medicinal substances among rural population of 'Paite tribe' and identify the various factors that impede their use.
- To capture the dynamics of the interaction and changes that has occurred in relations to utilization of indigenous medicinal substances and tribal medical practitioners.
- To explore the changes in tribal medicine with introduction of allopathic/modern medicine.
- To examine the changes in structure of provisioning and how it had influenced the health seeking behaviour of the community.

ORGANISATION OF BOOK

This present book has been organized in the following chapters :

Chapter 1 - Indigenous Medicine and Health care : An Overview. This chapter introduces the research question and the perspective of the study. It explains the concept of the study. It also states the rationality behind choosing the study areas and the objectives of the study.

Chapter 2 - Evolution and Trade in Indigenous Medicine: Reviewing its Impact on Health. This chapter brings out the social, political, economic and cultural factors that affect the evolution of indigenous medicine. It also discusses the roles played by international agencies of the developed countries in regard to promoting indigenous medicine for their own benefits and how trade trends in medicinal plants had an impact on the public health of developing countries.

Chapter 3 - Research Design. This chapter presents the methodology of the study. It discusses the scientific rationality on why the study area was selected. It also explains the tools and techniques used in collecting data, the research processes etc. and the limitation faced while conducting the study.

Chapter 4 - Profile of the study area. This chapter introduces the profile of the study area beginning from the State to the village.

Chapter 5 - Health, Disease and Care Utilization. This chapter discusses the profile of the study population, which includes their socio-demographic and economic profiles, utilization pattern of health care services, types of diseases found and their perception of disease causation. Their resort pattern for any treatment is also discuss using tables and figures.

Chapter 6 - Summary and Conclusion. This chapter summarises the whole studies and draws inferences from the findings of the field study and the review of literature. It also gives suggestions concluded from the inferences. Then it concludes the study by giving a few recommendations for policy makers.

NOTES

1. Census of Manipur, 2001, "Of the thirteen major STs, Hmar has recorded the highest literacy of 79.8 per cent, followed by Paite (79%), Any Mizo (Lushai) tribes (74%), Anal (73.9%), and Tangkhul (72.7%)".
2. Census of Manipur, 2001, 'In the age group of 5-14 years, 69.2 per cent of the SΓ population is attending schools or any other educational institutions. Of the thirteen major STs, Paite has recorded the highest 79.9 per cent, closely followed by Tangkhul (77.9%), Hmar (73.9%), Anal (71.9%), and Kom

(71.3%). Thadou (60.5%) has the lowest percentage attending school in the age group of 5-14 years.'

REFERENCES

Banerji, D. and Anderson, S. 1982. "A Sociological study of the awareness of symptoms suggestive of pulmonary tuberculosis", *Bulletin of WHO,* 23.

Bodekar, Gerard. 1994. "Traditional Health Care and Public Policy: Recent Trend", *Workshop paper, IDRC,* pp. 96-108.

Bose, Asish and Desai. 1983. *Studies in social dynamics of primary health care,* Hindustan Publishing Corporation (India), Delhi.

Census of India 2001, Manipur, Series 14 (provisional population totals), Directorate of Census Operations, Manipur.

Datta, S K. 2001. "Marketing of Wild Medicinal Plants Tribal Economy in India", *Economic and Political Weekly,* September 22, pp. 3598-3602.

Hazra, Jayati. 2002. "Health and Development of North East India", *Geographical Review of India,* Vol. 64, No 1, pp. 21-32.

Helly, Jason and Kiran Cherla. 1999. *Medicinal plant sector in India: A review,* Bookwell Publisher, New Delhi, p. 59.

Hufford, J. David. 1997. "Folk Medicine and Health Culture in Contemporary Society", *Complementary and Alternative Therapies in Primary Care,* Vol. 24, No.4, December, pp.723-741.

Lee, Rance P.L. 1982. "Comparative Studies of Health Care Systems", *Social Science and Medicine,* Vol. 16, pp. 629-642.

Mukhopadhya, Alok (ed). 1997. *Report of the Independent Commission on Health in India,* Voluntary Health Association of India, pp. 76-77.

Mukhopadhya, Alok. 1992. "*Indigenous Health Services—The State of the Art*", State of India's Health, Voluntary Health Association of India, New Delhi.

Pedersen, Duncan and Veronica Baruffati. 1989. "Healers, Deities, Saints and Doctors: Elements for the analysis of medical systems", *Social Science and Medicine,* Vol. 29, pp. 487-496.

Segismundo, Ma Chona L. 1994. "Traditional Health Systems: Challenges in the Philippines", *Workshop Paper, IDRC,* pp.100-114.

Shankar, Darshan and S.N Venugopal. 2000. "Malaria: The Indigenous Understanding and Management", *Amruth,* April, pp. 17-22.

WHO. 1978. *Primary Health Care,* A joint report by the Director-General of the World Health Organization and the Executive Director of the United Nations Children's Fund, Geneva-New York.

Zhang, Xiaorui. 1994. "WHO's Policy and Activities on Traditional Medicine", *Workshop paper, IDRC,* pp.139-142.

2

Evolution and Trade in Indigenous Medicine

Reviewing Its Impact on Health

Long relegated to marginal status in health planning in developing countries, indigenous medicine or more appropriately indigenous systems of health care have undergone a major process of revival in the past two decades or more. An emerging international policy climate has seen new recognition given to the efficacy, affordability and sustainability of many of these local traditions of health and medicine.

In this section evolution of indigenous medicine is discussed and illustrated with experiences from countries of Asia, Africa and the Americas, with special focus on the Indian experience. Some of the models of health care pluralism and World Health Organization's policy and activities on Primary Health Care will be discussed. Lastly, an effort will be made to understand relevance of indigenous medicine in primary health care and the latest source of influence on the promotion of indigenous medicine, i.e. a rush by some multinationals to patent and market products of indigenous medicine. Such recent developments have brought forth a plethora of issues, and at the same time, ushered in a new era for indigenous medicine.

EVOLUTION OF INDIGENOUS MEDICINE

The indigenous medicine of different countries and cultures vary from one another in regard to formal recognition. While in most parts of Asia particularly in China or in Indian subcontinent, indigenous medicine is recognized as formal system of medicine. While in most African and South American countries such recognition is missing. This differential evolution of indigenous medicine can be traced back to the differential nature of colonialism that countries around the world had to endure. Apart from brutal incursions from imperial Japan, the Chinese belt of Asia remained largely unscathed by colonialism. India, Pakistan, Bangladesh, on the other hand endured, almost 200 years of British Raj.

Evolution of indigenous medicine in India

Before the British, the Moghuls came from Central Asia to conquer India, settled in, and ruled it as rather benevolent rulers. The Moghuls not only brought a rich cultural heritage of their own, but also contributed immensely in further cultural, social and economic development in India. Under the Moghul rule the Indian indigenous medicine (Kabiraji, Ayurvedic, Siddha, etc.) received royal encouragement to flourish. The Unani system came through the Muslims who settled in India during the Moghul rule. Surprisingly, these indigenous medicinal systems acquired and retained to this day, a religious orientation – Unani by Muslims, while Kabiraj/Ayurvedic by Hindus. By the time the British came, these systems were quite developed, with their own schools and formularies. The religio-ethnic groups identified so strongly with one or other of those systems that the British found it difficult to ignore them, even when they were looked upon with disdain. Between 1757 and 1835, the new colonial power tolerated the indigenous medical systems, while laying the foundation for the Western medical system (Islam, 1994).

It is customary to see 1835 as a major turning point in British attitudes to Indian culture. This was the year of Macauley's Minute on educational policy, where he argued that European culture should provide the curriculum of schools and colleges. While this move had obvious significance, it does not mean a total ban on the teaching of indigenous medical aspects nor on cooperative relationships between the British Raj and the indigenous practitioners as a class. Nevertheless, the social, political and geographical reality of India made the British adopt an attitude of benign neglect towards the indigenous medical systems. Prior to the establishment of the Indian Sanitary Commission in 1860s there was no commitment by the state to provide health care services for its citizen, and there was a slow extension of that commitment beyond plague control and the provision of dispensaries. There was an awareness of the strength of the indigenous groups: plans to introduce medical registration in the 1880s were dropped because the Western doctors were too weak to defeat the expected hostility from the *vaids* and the *hakims* (Jeffery, 1982).

A change to greater hostility can be dated from about the end of the century. By this time the cream of the Western doctors in India – the Indian Medical Service, (recruited in Britain though 5% Indians by1913) – was more conscious of its claims to a scientific legitimation. The early twentieth century saw considerable political conflict as the rising bourgeois nationalist movement embraced the idea of science. The Indian National Congress included leading indigenous practitioners in its rank as well as modernizers like Nehru.

As Indians gained positions in Ministries after 1919 they were expected to implement policies based on the general view that the indigenous practitioners will constitute the medical attendants of by far the largest portion of the Indian community for many years to come. But their scope was limited by severe financial restrictions and their impact was further reduced by pressures from the Indian Medical Services, whose members provided the senior medical civil servants. The new Legislative Councils supported the 'Indian' systems of medicine on both patriotic and economy grounds; but Ministers in several provinces resisted this and used their limited funds to attempt tc bring 'modern scientific medicine and surgery within reasonable reach of all', spending only small sums on research into the indigenous systems and for improved training. As a result, relatively a few indigenous medical colleges were given state patronage; the scheme of medical registration excluded those who had not received Western medical training; and the Government of India restricted its activities to an investigation into the pharmacopoeia of indigenous drugs (Jeffery, 1982).

One of the most obvious ways in which the Congress governments after 1947 followed the precedents established by the British Raj in the sphere of health policies. The Bhore Committee's report (established by the British to plan for the reconstruction after the Second World War was over) was adopted instead of the report of National Planning Committee (established by Congress itself in 1938). On relationships with the indigenous healers both the reports were ambivalent, but Bhore was more hostile. The N.P.C. resolved that "*An attempt should be made to absorb the practitioners of the Ayurveda and Unani systems of medicine into the State health organization by giving them further scientific training where necessary. Medical training in every field should be based on scientific method.*" By contrast the Bhore report pointed out that the indigenous systems had nothing to say about public health, preventive medicine, obstetrics or advanced surgery, and described the systems as archaic and outside the onward march of world science. Bhore's policies involved *a country-wide extension of a system of medicine which in our view, must be regarded as neither Eastern nor Western but as a corpus of scientific knowledge and practice belonging to the whole world and to which every country has made its contribution.*

By 1947, then, it was possible to discern three main organized groups contesting the medical domain in India: the cosmopolitan doctors, with a stranglehold on the medical bureaucracy; the 'pure' indigenous practitioners, and the integrated practitioners. True to its 'soft state' approach, the political leadership of the country paid lip service to the indigenous systems of medicine and they were never taken seriously. A very half-hearted and obviously superficial efforts were made to conduct research to rediscover their lost heritage and to promote further growth and development in this systems of medicine (Banerji, 1979). Going in tune with these developments towards the indigenous medicine the majority of Indians have lost enthusiasm and value to be given to indigenous medicine. Their response to major medical problems was very much in favour of the Western (Allopathy) system of medicine, irrespective of social, economic, and occupational considerations. Availability of such services and ability of patients to meet the expense were the two major constraints.

A brief account of other countries

Like India, Pakistan and Bangladesh gave recognition and State patronage to their indigenous systems of medicine, only after independence. It was in 1962 that Pakistan first enacted the Unani and Ayurvedic Medical Practitioners Act to recognize and regulate these traditional health systems. In China, the post-revolutionary governments also contributed to continued development of these indigenous medical systems in the Indian subcontinent and China. As early as in 1955, a few years after the revolution, the Chinese Government emphasized the need to promote indigenous medicine (Islam, 1994).

The African countries went through a different kind of colonialism as compared to other developing countries. It suffered from the indignity of slavery, apartheid, most extreme form of repression and oppression. When slaves were not treated as humans, there was no question of providing any respect for their culture. Thus there was least or no respect for their health practices and products. On the contrary they were repressed, often brutally. The colonizers did not know that indigenous medicines are effective in curing many illnesses. They believed that the indigenous healers were just a rogue and a deceiver who prevented many patients, who would otherwise be treated effectively with modern drugs and surgery, from reaching government hospitals and mission hospitals. Their belief that indigenous healers encourage witchcraft "which was the way of Christian missionary work", also played a role in this policy of suppression (Islam, 1994). So unlike their Asian counterparts, the African indigenous medicine did not enjoy a natural process of evolution and development. It remained undeveloped, neglected and unrecognized. Consequently, African indigenous stagnated, and often, further degenerated during the long period of colonial rule.

A different kind of colonialism prevailed in the Americas, Australia and New Zealand. In those places, colonialism was physical and permanent. The Aborigines were physically uprooted and annihilated. A new society was created on the ashes of the old. The European settlement and parallel policy of "replacement of the Natives" were so efficient that "by the early 1800s few Native Americans remained east of the Mississippi river" and "by the beginning of this twentieth century, the vanishing Americans numbered only about 250,000 in the United States." The indigenous population of Mexico decreased from 2.3 million in 1650 to about one million in 1890s (Islam, 1994).

Thus little can be expected from such colonialism. Quite obviously, this brand of colonialism had scant respect for the culture of the vanquished. Health practices and products of the indigenous people of the Americas, therefore, remained unrecognized and unexplored. It not only suffered from lack of a natural growth, but also faced the spectre of total extinction along with the annihilation of its adherents. Unlike the Africans or the Asians, the Natives did not regain independence, but struggled with continued discrimination, segregation and socio-political isolation. Not surprisingly these indigenous medicine of different countries is perhaps one of the most endangered cultural heritage of modern times. Some of the indigenous knowledge is fast disappearing, and is likely to extinct, if not preserved immediately. Preserving and further developing indigenous health practices and products must be regarded as great challenges of our time.

MODELS OF HEALTH CARE PLURALISM

Different types of relationship can exist between biomedicine and indigenous medicine. This clarification is important as there has been a numerous publications on the advantages and problems in incorporating healing traditions into modern health care delivery systems, following the Alma Ata declaration of 1978, which advocated utilizing indigenous healers to help deliver primary health care. This will involve creating a typology, which emphasizes two variables:

(1) The relationship between biomedicine and indigenous healing traditions in terms of cultural equality (legal recognition and access to resources), and

(2) The nature of interaction between biomedicine and indigenous healing traditions (intolerance, collaboration, etc.). Health care pluralism can be understood as a system embracing many minority groups and cultural traditions.

Types of relationship

(1) Intolerant Orthodoxy

In this type, biomedicine has a monopoly on health care and uses its power base to prevent alternative healing traditions from obtaining legal status. In societies in which biomedicine has this kind of power, it is referred to as orthodox system and all other systems are considered as unorthodox. For example, it was not many years ago that colonial powers persecuted indigenous healers in Africa (Neumann and Lauro, 1982) and socialist countries such as the Russia and Cuba decided that only modern scientific medicine would be allowed (Pedersen and Baruffati, 1989).

This type of intolerance usually did not eliminate indigenous healing traditions but simply forced them underground. Many indigenous healing traditions lost their positions of "structural superiority", but they did not necessarily lost their "functional strength" (Lee, 1982). Therefore, we can say that although this type of intolerant orthodoxy may be characterized by unofficial medical pluralism, relations between biomedicine and indigenous healing traditions are characterized by structural inequality and intolerance on the part of the biomedical practitioners.

(2) Tolerant orthodoxy

In this type, as in the type of intolerant orthodoxy, there is a single orthodox healing traditions, but many of its practitioners are tolerant of alternatives traditions. In an attempt to provide culturally appropriate health care, tolerant orthodox practitioners made an effort to understand the beliefs and behaviours of minority patients. This type of tolerant is characteristics of what has been called the "multicultural health care" movement in North America.

It is important to note, however, that in societies characterized by tolerant orthodoxy, alternative healing traditions are accorded legal status. Unofficial health care practices exists in practice, and may even be encouraged, but a single tradition (biomedicine) controls official health care policy and training and licensing of legally-recognized practitioners. In other words, despite its tolerance, biomedicine retains its position of structural superiority.

(3) Parallel independent traditions

In this type rather than a single orthodox system, there are two or more traditions that are legally recognized. Although patients have freedom of choice, there is little active collaboration among practitioners of different traditions. A good example exists in our country, India itself, where traditional and biomedical clinics exist side by side. Patients frequently go to the traditional clinic for what they consider to be traditional diseases, and to the biomedical for diseases considered modern. Although traditional healers may borrow some of the 'trappings' of biomedicine (such as white coat) in order to achieve greater responsibility, there is usually little cooperation between the personnel of traditional and biomedical clinics.

However, in this type of parallel independent traditions, official medical pluralism does not necessarily imply structural equality. In fact, biomedicine usually is in a position of structural superiority in that it tends to be favoured by government officials, many of whom have been trained in the West and may view their own indigenous traditions as backward or even superstitious. A relation among practitioners of biomedicine and indigenous medicine is generally characterized by indifference, and the choice of what kind of healer to utilize for a particular condition is left to the patient. In brief, parallel independent traditions, have official health care pluralism, but at least in terms of interaction among health care practitioners, it is of passive type.

(4) Collaboration and combination

In this type, the practitioners of two or more legally recognized healing traditions engaged in active collaboration, resulting in a combination of therapeutic techniques, or else the beliefs, practices and medicine of two or more traditions are combined by a single individual. Perhaps the most common type of collaboration is for healers from different traditions to refer patients to each other, depending upon the ailment, or for indigenous healers to be included in the official health care system in those parts of the country in which members of their own ethnic group predominate. A very good example of this model is in China where "interdisciplinary" teams can consist of biomedical personnel, traditional Chinese medicine practitioners, and even personnel trainéd in one of the minority traditions such as Mongolian or Tibetan medicine.

This model of collaboration and combination includes a range of options, which provide for active collaboration among practitioners of different healing traditions and/ or combination of different therapeutic techniques and medicine within the same practice. This more active type of health care pluralism from parallel independent tradition model which may also expose a patient to different techniques and medicines, but without the cooperation, or even knowledge, of the practitioners involved.

(5) Integration

In this type, the goal is to synthesize the theory and practice of different healing traditions into a more comprehensive system. This goes beyond collaboration among practitioners from different traditions, or combining different techniques in a single practice. China is perhaps the best example of this policy. However, since philosophical underpinnings of the indigenous and Western medical systems are quite different and often contradictory, real integration is extremely difficult, if not impossible. At the same time, a policy to combine two or more system in which there is power disequilibria among the partners can not lead to integration in the true sense of the term. In such a scenario one may end up dominating the other. In such cases, perhaps establishing equity is more important than integration (Young, 1994).

INDIGENOUS MEDICINE AND PRIMARY HEALTH CARE

In the 1970s there have been an attempt to re-evaluate indigenous practices and to encourage the collaboration between indigenous and modern medicine. These attempts have been promoted in some cases by the 'nationalist' movements to rescue indigenous medicine, or simply as a strategy for extending health care coverage at low cost. These initiatives have received support and have been encouraged by adoption of the resolutions by governments at international level, as in the WHO. It stated that, "the members state of WHO are engaged in preparing and implementing strategies for the attainment of health for all by the year 2000, if a level of health that will permit them to lead a socially and economically productive life, a goal popularly known as Health for All by the year 2000. To succeed in attaining this goal, all useful methods will have to be employed and all possible resources mobilized. Among these methods are various kinds of indigenous practices, and among those resources are various types of indigenous practitioners and birth attendants." He also stated "this approach was endorsed by the International Conference on Primary Health Care, held in Alma Ata in 1978. The declaration of Alma Ata described primary health care and referred to the need for a variety of health workers, including indigenous practitioners as needed, who are suitably trained socially and technically to work as health team and to respond to the expressed needs of the community" (Mahler, former Director General of WHO, 1983). Indigenous medicine was incorporated in 1976.

As per its declaration towards Primary Health Care, the WHO has taken up various initiatives concerning indigenous medicine. A series of standards and guidelines, guide books or booklets on the proper use of medicinal plants, both based on local experience and modern scientific research in order to ensure the proper and safe use of indigenous remedies, have been issued by the WHO headquarters and regional offices. Comprehensive training programmes for indigenous healers, medical doctors and other professional health workers have been carried out for several years in some developing countries (Zhang, 1994).

There is no doubt that WHO is putting its effort, energy and resources in promoting indigenous medicine for primary health care needs. However, it seems that a little progress has been made in actually utilizing indigenous health practitioners or in improving indigenous medicinal substances. It appears in fact that in entire developing countries there are only one or two countries in which indigenous healers and their medicines are actually incorporated in the national health care system. Thus, a question remain—if the policy is there, why then is it so little implemented and how should outcome be evaluated when it is so?

First of all, it is important to recognize that every culture has its own characteristic health care system. The foundational theories, concepts and principles upon which indigenous health science is based are different from Western medical science. For example, in India Ayurveda has evolved as a comprehensive health care system. It addressed itself to health and disease and does not treat disease independent of facts like food habits, occupation and life styles. On the other hand we have the modern medicine, which conceptualized the patient as the sum of a finite set of subsystems, which in turn have to be seen for therapeutic purposes as a relatively and functionally autonomous of each other. It is basically based on the germ theory. Besides these major differences, the basic question the indigenous systems of medicine had to confronted was the scientificity. More or less, one reason that hamper the WHO target to achieve health for all, can be attributed to this kind of unnecessary debate on the theories, concepts etc., questioning the scientificity of indigenous medicine, also it diverted the goal and purpose behind WHO resolution. Arguing it more strongly on the whether indigenous medicine is a science or not, one can argue that, "if science is defined as a body of knowledge obtained by a systematic observation of events, it cannot be denied that such observations had been carried out in the past as well. There is nothing in the definition of science or the scientific method, which precludes the possibility of referring back to scientific insights obtained in the past or in other cultures. Indian system of medicine by this definition certainly qualifies to be a science in its own right" (Ramprasad, 1994).

Secondly, we have seen WHO's policies in giving training to the indigenous healers as a part of integrating them into the national health care system. However, integration of health system raises critical question from modern experts, on the multiple type of drugs, multiple type of practitioners, types of training and how does the planner, administrator of policy maker deal with this plurality. Primary health care has been defined at the international conference of WHO and UNICEF as, "essential health care made universally accessible to individuals and families in the community by means acceptable to them, through their full participation and at a cost that the community and the country can afford. Primary health care addresses to:

- The main health problems in the community,
- Includes education concerning prevailing health problems and the methods of prevention and controlling them,
- The promotion of food supply, proper nutrition, adequate and safe water supply, basic sanitation, and
- Rely at local and referral level on health workers including physicians, nurses, midwives as well as indigenous practitioners to work as a team (WHO & UNICEF, 1978).

WHO has given this definition in the most ideal form as possible. But if some of these aspects of primary health care have to be a reality a few question needs to be given a serious thought.

- How will primary health care be integrated with traditional system of health care?
- If the government is serious about what is envisaged, will it be possible to allocate budget to strengthen integration?
- Can the existing health care system able to support primary health care by referral, supervision, supplies and transportation to patients? And

- Can the practices of indigenous system be given the status it deserves as being holistic, not as mere treatment with medicinal plants alone?

Besides the above questions, we also need to look into the background of indigenous while attempting integration of indigenous and modern medicine. For example, healers always practice in suspicion with a feeling of insecurity. How do we safeguard the interest of such healers who are not recognized and belong to acceptable system of health care? When we are concerned about the legal control of malpractice within the indigenous system we also fail to take into account the self-regulated modes of practices that existed in the earlier days. For example, it is recalled that ageing healers get distinct signal as their power recede. An incident happened when an old man treated his patient for scorpion bite and sent him home. The patient and his relatives however returned in an hour saying that the pain had resurfaced. The old man at once understood that some one else was challenging his powers and that he was incapable of retaliating. He sent the patient home with apologies and sat down quietly for a long while. Then all of a sudden he asked his twenty-five years old son if he wanted to inherit the power. The son was happy and become the successor on the subsequent eclipse night. There are also many other examples where the healers had an inborn talent to cure and diagnose diseases. With such kind of background an indigenous healer may be uncomfortable to work in a setting totally different from they are past oriented.

How do we cope with the kind of training that was pursued by the indigenous healers to pass on their powers? Sometimes the healers choose their successors. Can this type of training be envisaged? These examples are cited only to briefly mention on the kind of problems one can encounter in attempting to integrate the indigenous systems along with the formal system. Therefore, WHO have to reconsider the kinds of assistance and approaches offered to the primary health care in developing countries.

Besides some of these managerial problems of integration, there are other valid issues. As the market incorporates the products of indigenous systems of medicine, the resource base of these systems, of communities and their rights over it, are further expropriated. The crisis in the forms of knowledge, practice, and organization of indigenous people, health care deepens further.

'Health for All by the year 2000' was a slogan at the time of Alma Ata declaration. But in today's burgeoning crisis of development and health care, health for all seems to be a dream of the distant past.

RECENT TRADE TRENDS IN MEDICINAL PLANTS

Medicinal plants not only intersect with the areas of health but also covers a broader area related to the national economy. In terms of the volume and value of medicinal plants exported, India ranks second in the world. Data on exports of medicinal plants from India over the years 1990-91 to 1993-94, consolidated by Agricultural and Processed Food Products Development Authority of the Ministry of Commerce lists 21 commodity groups (Ved, 1997).

In this section we will examine the trade related issues at the local, national and international level. The fact that medicinal plants are living resources, exhaustible if overused and sustainable if used with care, is little understood by traders, agents and official concerned, while for the local people involved in the trade it is all about daily bread. In India it is estimated that collection and processing of medicinal plants contributed to at least 35 million workdays of employment annually to the poor and underemployed workforce. According to the Bhopal based National Centre for Human Settlements and the Environment, 50 million people live in and around forest areas and rely on NTFP (Non-timber forest products) for survival (Down to Earth, 2001).

It is not only an income generating activity for the herb gatherers, but it is also important to note that extraction of medicinal plants is a job of necessity rather than of choice, and that it may be a standby until more profitable means of making a living are available, particularly through livestock and agricultural activities. However, as these products (medicinal plants) become more valuable, access tend to be monopolized by the richer segments of the society while the poor forest-dwellers lose access to the resources. This leaves most of the community of herb gatherers at the mercy of the traditional moneylenders turned primary herb traders. The agent sets his trap by offering a loan whenever they needed and usually repay it through the sale of medicinal plants. Sometimes to pay back the loans and the interest too, the gatherers go deeper into the forests. In spite of their hard labour and efforts, survey reveals that the tribal people get a paltry one-tenth of what the agent actually gets from the traders (*Down to Earth*, 2001). Such kind of discrimination occurs because of the complexity and secrecy in the trade of medicinal plants. A typical chain of such transaction starts with the collection of these plant materials in the wild, through tribals and villagers, including women and children, followed by a local level consolidation of these collections by a network of local traders/ handlers and delivery at "road-head" centres. The material collected at such road-head centres then flows down to the local and regional wholesale markets, the latter generally located in bigger towns or cities. Such chains of transactions in the medicinal plants trade involve a very large number of collectors, processors and handlers, commission agents/ middlemen and carriers (Amruth, 1997).

Thus, at the national and sub-national level, the current disorganized and illegal forms of trade in medicinal plants benefit only traders and agents. The local people and the practitioners of medicinal plants want a change in the system, in the form of government intervention. Cultivation of medicinal plants offered, as the sound option by the government does not help the local people eventually. It may be beneficial for the rich farmer who can take the risk in such an uncertain market environment. However, it is a lucrative business involving high risk for the poor farmer. They would be unable to benefit in view of the high inputs required to sustain productivity, as similar to the situation of what the poor farmers were facing due to the Green Revolution (Amruth, 1997). Medicinal plants cultivation, thus, may meet bulk industrial requirement and benefit large farmers, would be unable to benefit rural communities and may actually impoverish the tribal and forest side people.

IMPACT OF TRADE TRENDS ON HEALTH

For the vast majority of our rural people the conservation and sustainable use of medicinal plants is intimately linked to meeting their basic health care needs. Historically the use of this enormous medicinal plants diversity has been need based and was therefore large sustainable. It was the commercialization of indigenous medicine and the growth in exports that led to severe decline in the resource base. *The most damning impact has been on the role of medicinal plants/indigenous medicine in public health. While the market for indigenous medicine has expanded, its presence in the public health system has shrunk. The government has made no concerted attempt to ensure production of affordable, quality medicine to counter market trends. It has become more market friendly than people friendly.* The idea behind encouraging manufacturing companies to get into indigenous medicine was to make them available at a low price to those who could not afford expensive modern medicines. The aim of public health system was to extend the choice of alternatives to those who did not have any to begin with. Unfortunately after fifty years of independence, both the public health system and the markets have failed a majority of people in the country (M. Banerjee, 2000).

GLOBAL TRADE IN MEDICINAL PLANTS

In the last decade or so we can trace three developments, which though unrelated, have significantly affected the Indian medicine sector. (i) The Indian economy has changed tracks in terms of its orientation towards international economy and has become 'liberalized'. (ii) A new wave in the international economy, 'globalization' in the short hand of our times, has created a new trading regime, the World Trade Organisation. (iii) There is a renewed surge of interest in indigenous people's medicine in Europe and North America (M. Banerjee, 2000).

Indigenous medicine is viewed by the pharmaceutical industries as a source of "qualified leads" in the identification of bioactive agents, which can be synthetically modelled for the production of patented modern drugs. The National Institute of Health in the United States has initiated two drug discovery projects along these lines — one in 1992 from the National Cancer Institute, the National Heart Lung and Blood Institute and the National Institute of Mental Health and the other in 1993 from the National Institute of Allergies and Infectious Diseases (Bodekar, 1994). These projects promote a drug discovery model, which uses the skills of custodians of indigenous knowledge in identifying medicinal plants.

This recent development towards indigenous medicine raises concern towards intellectual property rights of the indigenous people where the wealthy countries are trying to steal from them. Lets try to see how all this began.

World Trade Organisation

As mentioned earlier there is a new wave in international economy where a new trading regime has been created under the World Trade Organisation popularly known as WTO. Most nations are bound by the rules of General Agreement on Tariffs and Trade (GATT) established in 1946 and superseded by the WTO in 1995. All the members countries automatically became the members of WTO as a result of acceptance of the Uruguay Round agreement and submission of commitments on trade in goods and services. The Organization currently has 135 nation members. The WTO sets the rules for the world trade in goods and services, adjudicates trading disputes between nations and punishes by levying fines and imposing sanctions to those nations that transgress these rules. Nations with WTO membership have access to markets, but access is a double-edge sword, as countries seeking admission must ensure that their markets are accessible to other WTO members as well (Ostry, 2001).

The Trade Related Aspects of Intellectual Property Rights (TRIPS) 1994 which is a part and parcel of WTO set-up binds all the members of WTO which seeks to reduce distortions and impediments to international trade (Mishra, 2001). It covers copy right and related rights, trade marks, geographical indications of source, industrial designs, patents, topographies of integrated circuits, protection of trade secrets and control of restrictive trade practices in licensing agreements. Part II, Section 5 of the TRIPS Agreement consisting of eight articles (Articles 27 to 34) applies to patents (Patni, 2001). Among those covered under TRIPS, patent will be discussed in detail, as it is more related to indigenous medicine and its basic ingredients that is medicinal plants.

The word 'patent' is derived from the Latin term 'petere' that means 'to open'. It signifies a record of grant made by the government of the patentee, which is open for the world. A patent, most simply explained, is a monopoly granted to a person who has either invented a new and useful article or made an improvement of an existing article or invented a new process of making an article. The rights of a patent holder include the right to make, sell, use, offer for sale, export and licence. A patent is granted by a legal system like the national law (the Indian Patent Act) — which would hold well within the country or regional law (like the European Patent Treaty) — which would hold well in subscribing to the treaty or the global law (like WIPO) — which would hold good worldwide. The grant of patent is conditional on its subject matter being disclosed and it is granted for a fixed period of time (Shiva & Bhutani, 2001).

Patent and indigenous medicine in India

In India the first act relating to Patent right was passed in 1856. Indian Patents and Designs Act followed this in 1911. The present Act (Patents Act, 1970) came into force on 20th April, 1972. Under the present Act, India recognizes only process patents, but not products patents. While WTO agreement requires both product and process patents in all fields. So India promulgated the Patents (Amendment) Ordinance on January 8, 1999 and will recognize product patent from January 1, 2005 (Shiva & Bhutani, 2001).

India's rich stock of indigenous medicine based on historical knowledge and traditional heritage has become an eyesore for transnational companies and other commercial outfits, which are engaged in biopiracy in the name of research and development and getting Indian indigenous medicine patented in their respective countries devoid of any international and national legal norms and ethical values. US Patent Office has become a heaven for multinational biopirators. There are number of items of Indian origin like Jamun, Gurmar, Turmeric, Basmati rice, Brinjal etc. which got patented in the US. This is the result of the law related to IPR (intellectual property rights), which encouraged illegal transfer of knowledge base from the communities in developing countries to the corporate houses of the developed countries for scientific analysis and creation of new products for global exploitation (Akhtar, 2001).

On the other hand, as already mentioned under the new patent regime information can be patented if the information is new and useful invention, invented by inventor and its details must be in written form. Moreover it is the invention, which can only be patented under the law. However, in the case of India's indigenous medicine, the discoveries and idea of patentability thereof is excluded as they are naturally occurring. Thus it can aptly be remarked that only inventions that are the product of inventive faculty of human beings are protected (Akhtar, 2001). Therefore, for the purpose of finding out whether the existing products and processes based on indigenous knowledge can be treated as invention, it is necessary to examine the meaning of the "new", "inventive step" and "industrial application". However the TRIPS Agreement has left them undefined.

The TRIPS agreement of GATT/WTO has globalize US-style patent laws. This has far reaching consequences and impacts not only on our capacity to provide for our basic needs of food and medicine, but also on the democracy and sovereignty. The universalization of patents to cover all subject matters, including life forms, has resulted in patents invading our forests and farms, our kitchens, and our medicinal plant gardens. Patents are now granted not just for machines but also for life forms and biodiversity; not just for new inventions but also for the knowledge of our grandmothers. This is tantamount to biopiracy. And contrary to popular perception, Western-style IPR systems, especially US patent laws, far from preventing intellectual piracy; seem to in fact promote it, even at times violating human rights (Shiva, 2001).

In a way, this can be viewed to be another form of neo-colonialism. Now the new gold is green. The wealthy countries are seen to be looking yet again at poorer countries as a source of raw materials to develop products for use in industrialized societies with profits going elsewhere than to the countries from where the initial material including the indigenous knowledge came.

A major concern is that this trend does not contribute to the development of indigenous medicine as a health care system for the poor and rural communities. Rather, it takes their medicinal knowledge and used it to serve the demand for new drugs in industrial countries, rather than for the treatment of malaria and other diseases, which decimate the populations of the developing countries. There is no attempt in most of the projects in developed countries using indigenous medicine, to develop a scientific understanding of the efficacy of the same medicinal plants in addressing the primary health care needs of the populations in the areas from which the plants derive.

Medicinal Substances in North East

North East India comprising seven states of Arunachal Pradesh, Assam, Manipur, Meghalaya, Mizoram, Nagaland and Tripura, known as seven sisters, portray a complex combination of factors, which has affected the health of a population in various ways. The region has remained relatively isolated and underdeveloped even after 50 years of independence, partly due to its location, and partly for the adherence of the people to their traditional lifestyle. Apart from the Brahmaputra valley, most of the North East consists of rugged terrain with hot, humid climate in the summer and cold, wet climate in the winter. The North East region is generally rich in biodiversity. It is among the world's most richest biodiversity region. Due to this diversity the people of North East enjoy better health conditions than other parts of India. Health ranks fifth among the indicators of well-being in terms of poor performance, but varies considerably within the states. Arunachal

Pradesh, Assam and Tripura record poor health while the eastern hill states of Manipur, Meghalaya and Nagaland enjoy better health conditions (Hazra, 2002). Health care facilities though poor in the North Eastern states of India is compensated by the low population densities and the existence of alternative tribal or folk medicine which survives on the medicinal plants and substances found in that region. Some of the medicinal substances found in this region are given in the appendices (Appendix I&II).

SUMMARY

In summary, we can see that indigenous medicine was born out of necessity and caters to the health care needs of the people since time immemorial. The differential evolution of different countries is traced from the kind of differential colonialism they faced. In India the evolution of indigenous medicine was traced in details from the Moghuls time till today. We can also state that through this evolution different types of models in health care began to exist. Hierarchical pluralism began to rule the health care system of many countries. The indigenous system of medicine was ignored and considered to be inferior to so called modern scientific medicine in many countries. In some countries it is recognized formally and existed side be side with the modern medicine as an alternative. With the WHO programme on indigenous medicine to be promoted for primary health care needs, the attention began to be shifted for improving the use of indigenous medicine and the practitioners due to its affordability and availability for the poorer masses, mostly in the developing countries. However, with the change in the global economic scenario (like the intellectual property rights and the issues of patenting, the new economic policy etc.) the main intention of promoting indigenous medicine seems to be diverted. It becomes more market oriented than people oriented. It is yet to be accorded its proper role with the overall health care system in developing countries.

In brief, this chapter brings out the social, political and economic factors that affect the evolution of indigenous medicine and the roles played by international agencies in promoting indigenous medicine and its impact on the public health care system of the developing countries. It also tries to present a bird's eyeview of the content of this study.

REFERENCES

Akhtar, Saleem. 2001. "New Patent Regimes: Protection of Indian's Heritage" In Koul, A.K. and Ahuja, V.K. (Ed) *The Law of Intellectual Property Rights: In Prospect and Retrospect*, Faculty of Law, University of Delhi, pp.103-112.

Banerjee, D. 1979. "Place of the Indigenous and the Western systems of Medicine in the health services of India", *International Journal of Health Services*, Volume 9, Number 3, pp. 511-519.

Banerjee, Madhulika. 2000. "Whither Indigenous Medicine", *Seminar*, 480, May, pp. 44-48.

Bodekar, Gerard. 1994. "Traditional Health Care and Public Policy: Recent Trend", *Workshop paper, IDRC*, pp.96-108.

Editorial. 1997. "Cultivation of medicinal plants — conservation charade", *Amruth*, August, pp.11-14 (Published by Foundation for Revitalization of Local Health Traditions).

Editorial. 2001, "Trading in contraband", *Down to Earth*, January, pp. 38-41.

Hazra, Jayati. 2002. "Health and Development of North East India", *Geographical Review of India*, Vol. 64, No. 1, pp. 21-32.

Islam, Anwar. 1994. "Understanding traditional health systems: A sociological perspective", *Workshop paper on traditional health system and public policy*, pp. 71-83.

Jeffery, Roger. 1982. "Policies towards Indigenous healers in Independent India", *Social Science and Medicine*, Vol. 16, pp. 1835-1841.

Lee, Rance P.L. 1982. "Comparative Studies of Health Care Systems", *Social Science and Medicine*, Vol. 16, pp. 629-642.

Mishra, D.N. 2001. "Evolution and Development of Intellectual Property Rights" In Koul, A.K and Ahuja, V.K. (Ed) *The Law of Intellectual Property Rights: In Prospect and Retrospect*, Faculty of Law, University of Delhi, pp. 49-51.

Ostry, S. Aleck. 2001. "International Trade Regulation and Publicly Funded Health Care in Canada", *International Journal of Health Services*, Vol. 31, No. 3, pp. 475-480.

Patni, P.K. 2001. "Patent System in India" In Koul, A.K. and Ahuja, V.K. (Ed) *The Law of Intellectual Property Rights: In Prospect and Retrospect*, Faculty of Law, University of Delhi, pp. 66-77.

Pedersen, Duncan and Veronica, Baruffati. 1989. "Healers, Deities, Saints and

Doctors: Elements for the analysis of medical systems", *Social Science and Medicine*, Vol. 29, No. 487-496.

Ramprasad, Vanaja. 1994. "Traditional Health Systems and Primary Health Care", *Workshop paper, IDRC*, pp.131-135.

Shiva, Vandana and Shalini Bhutani. 2001. An Activist Handbook on *Intellectual Property Rights and Patents*, Research Foundation for Science, Technology and Ecology.

Shiva, Vandana. 2001. *Patents—Myths and Reality*, Penguin Books, India.

Ved, D.K. 1997. "Trade in Medicinal Plants—The State of our Ignorance", *Amruth*, August, pp. 2-7.

WHO. 1978. *Primary Health Care,* A joint report by the Director-General of the World Health Organization and the Executive Director of the United Nations Children's Fund, Geneva-New York.

Young, David E. 1994. "Models of health care pluralism", *Workshop paper on Traditional Health System and Public Policy*, IDRC, pp. 62-70.

Zhang, Xiaorui. 1994. "WHO's Policy and Activities on Traditional Medicine", *Workshop paper, IDRC*, pp.139-142.

3

Research Design

INTRODUCTION

India's diverse agro-climatic zones, variation in regional topography, wide variations in flora and fauna has contributed to the richness of its biological diversity. Depending on the availability of principal medicinal plants, the country has been divided into eight phyto-geographic regions. They are the Western Himalayas, the Eastern Himalayas, North Eastern Region, Gangetic Plains, Semi-Arid Region, Western Ghats, Eastern Ghats, Andaman and Nicobar Islands. The principal medicinal and aromatic plants are found in these regions, which consist of their respective tribal population. In this study the focus is broadly on the North Eastern Region. In North East India, the majority of the medicinal plant species (70 per cent) occur in the forest areas and the remaining 30 per cent are found in non-forestlands including lands under cultivation (Datta, 2001). The tribal people and the forest dwellers collect a variety of leaves, fruits, seeds, nuts, roots, barks, tubers and rhizomes which have medicinal value. There has been a decrease in forest cover producing the wild medicinal plants in the tribal districts of North East India which may be due to irregular and unscientific collection, unscientific mining and quarrying, uncontrolled forest grazing, forest fires, shifting cultivation and biotic pressure beyond carrying capacity of the land (Datta, 2001).

Besides this problem, at the national and international level, marketing of medicinal plants faces serious problems. Trade in medicinal herbs, like any other natural product, suffers from market imperfections. Such imperfections are apparent both on supply side, as well as, on the demand side. Factors contributing to such market imperfections are: absence of a system of defining property rights; problems in arriving at a convincing patenting policy; unique characters of medicinal plants and uncertainty of their availability; knowledge of medicinal plants being restricted to a limited people; absence of organized market; interplay of middlemen etc.

Potential threat on the demand side of the market is from the piracy of indigenous knowledge and biological resources by both national and international companies and corporations engaged in the trade of phyto-medicines. Their interest in indigenous medicines of the developing countries is the main reason behind imperfections in trade. The World Trade Organisation allows signatory Countries to implement intellectual property rights over plant varieties. Such concessions made India's vast biological diversity of economically important plants more vulnerable for exploitation. In such a global scenario it is becoming more important to study the status of our indigenous medicine and to improve it through active participation of the local tribal people, and simultaneously by effective interventions of institutions in matters related to the demand management of medicinal herb. It is being said that with the present trend pointing towards an inexorable commercialization of the medicinal plant economy, there could be an emerging scenario where the rich alone would be able to afford herbal products. In the changing market scenario, let the tribal people have their due share.

SELECTION OF STUDY AREA

The study is conducted in Manipur. Manipur has nine districts, four in the plains and five in the hill region. The hill districts constitute only tribal population with no proper health facilities. Almost all the hill districts are overwhelmingly rural in character, few of them with headquarters depicting a semi-urban nature. Out of the five hill districts, Churachandpur district is selected because, according to the Census of Manipur, 2001, among the hill districts Churachandpur ranks first in terms of sex ratio and literacy among the hill districts. In Churachandpur district one sub-division, Thanlon was selected for the following reasons:

- Area of the Sub-Division and size of the population (19,209 in 1991 Census).
- Distances from the district headquarters (159 km from the district headquarters).
- Backwardness in terms of basic amenities (no power supply), as compared to other Sub-Divisions.
- Majority of the population belongs to Paite (the study tribe) (80 % of the district population).

It is assumed that remoteness and poor infrastructure would lead to use of indigenous medicinal substances.

Thanlon sub-division has 47 villages. Two villages were selected for the fieldwork. The two villages, namely Mualnuam and Thuangtam were selected for the following reasons:

- Mualnuam has almost all the basic amenities and had a population of around 1850, among one of the highest in the sub-division.
- Mualnuam ranks high in the amenities.
- Thuangtam, on the other hand, lacked basic amenities, even primary school.
- Thuangtam, has small population size and ranks low in the amenities index.
- The two villages at two ends of amenities scale were selected to examine if economic propensity made any difference in accessing a given type of health care.

SELECTION OF STUDY POPULATION

The field survey was based on a sample of 100 households selected to ensure that it is derived from the population in such a way as to represent different socio-economic status, demographic composition and environmental conditions in the two villages. The sample of 100 households was drawn from the list provided by the village Chiefs. The households were classified on the basis of their house type, as it signify status symbol in both the villages. Houses are divided into three types :

(1) Tin roof with wooden walls and floors— (High status)
(2) Thatched roof with wooden walls and floors —(Medium status)
(3) Thatched roof with bamboo walls and floors or mud floor — Low status.

The number of respondents from the sample of 100 households varies between 100 and 200, which means that one household does not necessarily have only one respondent. Efforts were made to select purposively, traditional healers, health care providers to be part of the respondents. Unfortunately there is only one respondent from traditional healer as they stop practicing for the past one decade. While regarding health personnel from the PHC, there was no one available in the village, as they prefer to reside in towns than in the village. They will come once or twice in the village when some targeted programme(s) is/are to be implemented.

RESEARCH METHODS

Tools and Techniques

The following tools and techniques were use during the course of research study :

Tools	*Techniques*
Questionnaire Schedule	Canvassing Questionnaire
Semi-structured Questionnaire	Key Informant Interviews
	In-depth Interviews
Field Notes	Case Studies
Check List	Focus Group Discussions
	Observations

The interview schedule was designed separately for the users, traditional healer and the health personnel. The questions were so formulated as to elicit all the relevant socio-economic, cultural, health seeking behaviour, utilization pattern and environmental parameters to be surveyed. It also included their response towards illnesses and the kind of treatment they resort to and their utilization pattern of the various system of medicine. Similarly the questionnaire for the traditional healers comprised questions on their socio-economic status, and the kind of practices and treatment healed by them, their opinion on the other system of medicine, their perception of their roles in the community. The questionnaire for the health personnel sought information about their perception of other system of medicine, types of illnesses found in the villages, responses of the community towards the services given in the health centre and towards the National Programmes.

The data was recorded in the questionnaire schedule. The open-ended interview schedules were used for the interviews. Each household interview took roughly 30-40 minutes. Some other methods used included group discussion, in-depth interviews, social mapping etc. with the intention to capture the real felt needs of the villagers. Observations of the village and the villagers were also recorded in the field diary.

To ensure good quality information, respondent's responses were recorded properly. The in-depth interviews with selected groups such as the Chief of the villages, committee or organizations directly concerned with the development of the village like the 'village development council' and personnel connected with health care delivery at the district and local level were also done. They were really useful for identification of the main problems in the village and at the District.

These responses were meaningful as the information was directly obtained from the community concerned and closely related to their problems and needs.

DATA SOURCE

The researcher used both the primary and secondary data. The primary data was collected using both qualitative and quantitative methods. The data was collected from the villagers/the common people, traditional healers and service providers in the health centre. Interview schedule/questionnaire, focus group discussion (FGDs) key-informant interviews, case studies, in-depth interviews and direct observations were the tools used in collecting primary data. It was collected during the months of December 2002 and January 2003. Besides the primary data, the researcher collected secondary data from published and unpublished data. In Manipur, the researcher consulted and collected information from various publications of the State government and Non-governmental organizations as well. Besides this, various publications of foreign government or international bodies and their subsidiary organizations are referred. Also journals, books, magazines and newspapers; reports and publications of various associations connected with the area of research study; reports prepared by research scholars, universities etc., are referred and consulted for collecting more information and to have strong theoretical orientation.

METHODS OF DATA COLLECTION

The study was done using both qualitative and quantitative methods. The field survey of about 100 respondents was used for the former and key informant interviews, in-depth interviews, case studies; focus group discussions were used for the qualitative analysis. After having selected the study population the questionnaire schedules (QSs) were canvassed to get the required information. In most cases, prior appointment was taken before actually canvassing the questionnaire schedule. In a day because of difficult terrain, it was possible to complete only few QSs.

RESEARCH PROCESS

Data Process

The collected data were processed in the following way —

- Editing-checking the QSs every evening and returning to the respondents for corrections/changes if any anomalies, gaps if any
- Coding the responses as per the themes of the question
- Classification for different sub-headings for different themes based on the SSQ checklist and field notes
- Tabulation for the purpose of explanation, according to chapters/sub-headings as the case may be
- Using percentages/rates/ratios (for quantitative data) for table

Data analysis and interpretation

The following indicators have been used in the analysis of the utilization pattern of indigenous medicinal substances:

- Socio-economic conditions
- Major health problems
- Physical factors
- Amenities available
- Resort pattern for treatment
- Preference for treatment
- Perception of the causes of illness
- Perception of the traditional healers and the health workers

LIMITATION OF THE STUDY

The major limitation was of not finding the traditional healers. In a survey of this nature, problems are bound to emerge. It was anticipated that the respondents would experience difficulty in recalling illness. In such a situation it was cross-checked with other respondents/family members and supplemented with literature. One of the main areas of uncertainty and ambiguity was the precise identification of illnesses. In instances of serious illnesses, the households possess hospital admission records and records of treatment given at the medical institutions; this also applies to immunization and visits to maternity homes and clinics. Reliance was placed on the respondents' ability to give a clear account of the illness. Problems with the traditional healer emerged in the same way as users. He has his own way of describing the kinds of illnesses he had treated, which give the researcher a problem in eliciting and classifying it in specific terminology. However, with the help of some school teachers and health workers the names of the illnesses could be translated to some extent. Some limitation is also faced in regard to secondary sources where the 2001 and 1991 Special tables on Scheduled Tribes of Manipur could not be located. So the study has to refer to 1981, even though it is two decades old.

REFERENCES

Datta, S. K. 2001. "Marketing of Wild Medicinal Plants Tribal Economy in India", *Economic and Political Weekly*, September 22, pp.3598-3602.

4

Profile of the Study Area

MANIPUR : AN INTRODUCTION

Manipur is a small hilly State in the Northeastern region of India. Its total area is 22,327 sq.km. Nagaland bound Manipur in the north, Mizoram in the south, and Myanmar in the east and Cachar district of Assam in the west (Map 4.1).

It was the illustrious late Pundit Jawaharlal Nehru who bestowed upon Manipur the solemn sobriquet it deserves, "A Jewel of India" and by Lord Irwin as the "Switzerland and of India." Indeed in is a sparkling jewel the glitter of which refuses to be dimmed by tempestuous tests of fire. The freshening features of its nature and the mesmerizing effects of its culture, is unfortunately, half hidden from the world.

Manipur came under the British rule in 1891. It was merged with the Indian Union in October 1949. Manipur became a full-fledged 'State of India' on the 21st January, 1972 as the 20th State of the Indian Union with 60-seat Legislative Assembly, out of which 19 are reserved for Scheduled Tribes and 1 for the Scheduled Castes. The people of Manipur elect two MPs for the Lok Sabha and one MP for the Rajya Sabha (DCHI, 1991).

Manipur is sharply divided into two cultural zones, the valley and the hills. The climate of Manipur is pleasant and healthy. The main crops in the State are paddy, maize, yam, and millets. The 29 tribes inhabit the hills that cover nine-tenths of the total area, and the valley by the 'Meiteis' who are in the majority (Liankhohau, 1994).

At present the total population of Manipur is 23,88,634 (RGI, 2001). The capital of Manipur is Imphal. There are nine districts in Manipur, which can be divided as hill and plain districts :

HILL DISTRICTS	*PLAIN DISTRICTS*
*CHURACHANDPUR**	IMPHAL EAST
CHANDEL	IMPHAL WEST
SENAPATI	THOUBAL
BISHNUPUR	TUKHRUL
TAMENGLONG	

* The study district.

The twenty-nine recognized tribes of Manipur could be roughly placed under two types — the Kuki-Chins and the Nagas (Appendix-I).

Also there are seven Scheduled Castes recognized. They are– (a) Dhupi/Dhobi, (b) Lois, (c) Muchi or Ravidas, (d) Namasudra, (e) Patni, (f) Sutradhar, (g) Yaithibi. The Plain districts are mainly occupied by the Scheduled Castes and the 'Meiteis'.

The hill districts of Manipur echo and reflect a different sound and sight. The majority are Christians by religion. Its inhabitants can easily pass off as locals of Hong Kong or Bangkok, but ironically invite a second look in our national metros. They are ethnic group reluctantly reconciled to their fate of being categorized by accident of history as Scheduled Tribes. But their outlook by and large, is global. Food habits tilt heavily on non-vegetarian delicacies.

Manipur is home to a host of species hard to spot elsewhere. Almost 67 per cent of the total geographical area of Manipur is hills covered by different types of forests. It is thus blessed with amazing varieties of flora and fauna. Depending upon the altitude of hill ranges, the climatic condition varies from tropical to sub-alpine. One came across wet forests and pine forests in different regions of the State and they together sustain a host of rare plants and animal species.

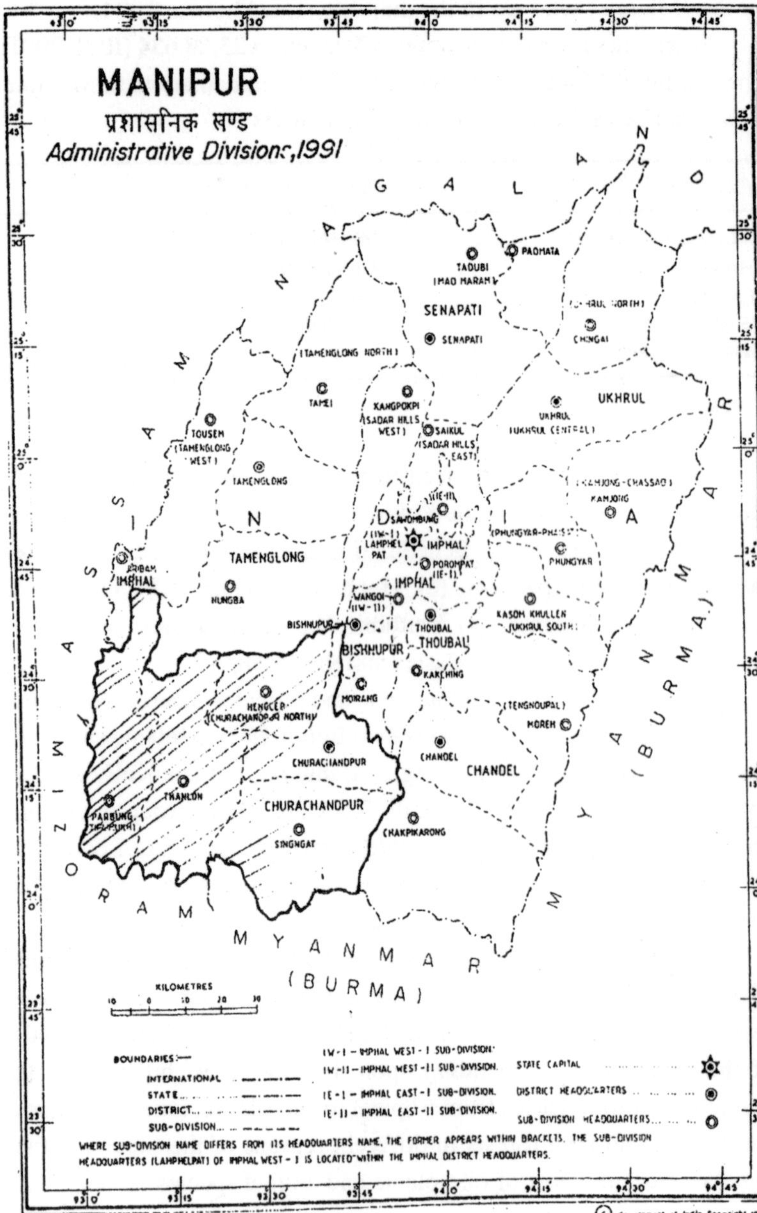

Based upon Survey of India map with the permission of the Surveyor General of India.

Map 4.1 : Map of Manipur

Health care system of Manipur

The state of Manipur has about 6.20 percent of North East India's population but does not have a matching share of medical facilities available at the national level [RGI, 2001, 33(i)]. There are fewer doctors and, therefore, large number of persons per doctor. There are fewer hospitals and dispensaries, fewer beds in the hospital. Besides, medical facilities are unevenly distributed. Big hospitals, equipments for specialized treatment, specialist etc. are all located in the urban centres. Broadly speaking, this is what the government has to say :

> "The state health department is fully committed in the total health care of its people in the spirit of health for all. The priority attention of the department is to provide the optimum health needs of the people in general and particularly to those living in rural and tribal areas of the state.
> The health system in the state of Manipur is based upon primary health care approach as envisaged in the National Health Policy of 1983 with the objective for attainment of 'Health for All' and 'All for Health".

A. *Administrative set-up of the Health services :*

(1) The administrative department or ministry located at the secretariat is at the highest level in the organization. A cabinet minister supported by a secretary/commissioner, joint secretary, deputy secretary and under secretary head it. Major decision concerning policies, programmes and proposals are taken at this level.

(2) The next level organization is the directorate of health services, which is the executive authority in regards to the health administration of the state. The director of health services who in turn is supported by additional director, joint director and deputy directors head it. The medical and health directorate gives direction and undertakes planning, organization, supervision, evaluation and monitoring of various health programmes.

(3) The district health administration is the third administrative unit and is headed by a chief medical officer (CMO) supported by a team of district level programme officers. The main activity of the district health administration is implementation, supervision, evaluation and monitoring of health programmes and delivery of health care services at the grassroots level through a network of primary health subcentre, primary health centre, community health centre etc. Referral services needing specialized treatment are provided by the CHCs and the district hospital. The department is actively considering strengthening of the health administration by developing subdivisional level health administrative units.

B. Health care delivery system

(1) Primary Care level comprises of sub-centre, primary health centre, community health centre. Essential basic health care is provided at this level.

(2) Secondary Care level CHCs and district hospital as referral centre where comparatively complex curative services are provided with basic specialist facilities.

(3) Tertiary Care level where specialist and super specialist care are provided. It includes the state level hospital (J.N. Hospital and RIMS).

C. Steps have been initiated and taken up to implement the strategies outlined in the National health policy within the framework of Five-year plans.

The state is well placed regarding the number of primary health service units established per population. However, the majority of the units are handicapped due to lack of full complement of requisite infrastructure. Many units were established without proper building and equipment and logistic support even as some units were made operational by redeployment of the existing manpower without post creation, thus compromising on the performance of the units from which the manpower has been diverted. Yet other units cannot be made fully functional due to want of skilled manpower/specialist despite post creation" [Government of Manipur: Health Department Annual Plan (2002-2003) and Tenth Five Year Plan (2002-2007)].

THE STUDY DISTRICT CHURACHANDPUR

The district of Churachandpur derives its name from the town of Churachandpur after Sir Churachand Singh, the Maharaja of Manipur. It lies on the southwestern part of Manipur between 24.0-degree north and 24.3 degree north latitude and 93.15 degree east and 94.0 degree east longitude (DCH Churachandpur, 1991).

Churachandpur district is bounded on the north by Tamenglong district, on the east by the district of Imphal and Chandel, on the south by Myanmar and Mizoram and on the west by the state of Mizoram and Assam (Map 4.2). The average altitude of the district is 914.0 metres above sea level. The area of the district as furnished by the Surveyor of India is 4570.0 sq.km (District Census Handbook of Manipur, 1991).

Historically the district is characterized by a stream of immigrants, mainly of the Kuki origin, from Burma and the Chittagong Hill Tracts (now in Bangladesh) beginning right from the 15th and 16th century even up to the early part of 20th century. Depending on the period of migration these Kuki immigrants have been classified by various authors into the old Kuki group and the new Kuki group. On the basis of their language and affinity to other social characteristics they are further classified into northern Chin subgroup and Kuki-Chin subgroup. They gradually spread throughout the district and other hilly areas of Manipur from various directions in search of new fertile and suitable habitation areas (DCH of Churachandpur, 1991).

The spread of Christianity among the different sections of the people in the district in the beginning of the 20th century is another epoch making achievement in the history of the district. From a small start the district now have a number of Christian organizations, missionaries operating in all the corners of the district. The spread of Christianity is still a continuing process.

Churachandpur district was previously known as South District. It came into existence, in the year 1969 as a result of district reorganization of Manipur. Till then it was a Union territory having ten sub-divisions. Now the district has five subdivisions and six tribal development blocks (T.D.Bs). Every subdivision, except Churachandpur subdivision has one T.D.Bs and, in these subdivisions, the jurisdiction of the T.D.Bs coincide with that of the respective subdivisions.

Subdivision	*Headquarters*	*T.D. Block*	*Headquater*
1. Tipaimukh	Parbung	1. Parbung	Parbung
2. Thanlon*	Thanlon	2. Thanlon	Thanlon
3. Churachand-pur North	Henglep	3. Henglep	Henglep
4. Churachandpur	Churachandpur	4. Churachandpur	Churachandpur
5. Singngat	Singngat	5. Samulamlan	Samulamlan
		6. Singngat	Singngat

* The study Subdivision

At present, the population of Churachandpur district is 228,707 and rank fifth in the State. It has a sex ratio of 993 and rank fourth in the State. It ranks sixth in terms of density of population with fifty persons per square kilometre. In terms of literacy it has improved from 58.17 (1991) to 74.67 (2001) and rank third in the State (Census on population of Manipur 2001).

Physiography, climate and natural resources of Churachandpur district

The whole of Churachandpur district is hilly and is covered with rough and uneven terrain. The hills attain greater elevations in the north and slopes towards the south. On the basis of geology, soil, climate, topography and natural vegetation the hills of the district have been divided by the office of the Registrar General of India into (1) the western hilly region covering the whole of Tipaimukh subdivision, (2) the eastern hilly region covering Churachandpur North, Churachandpur

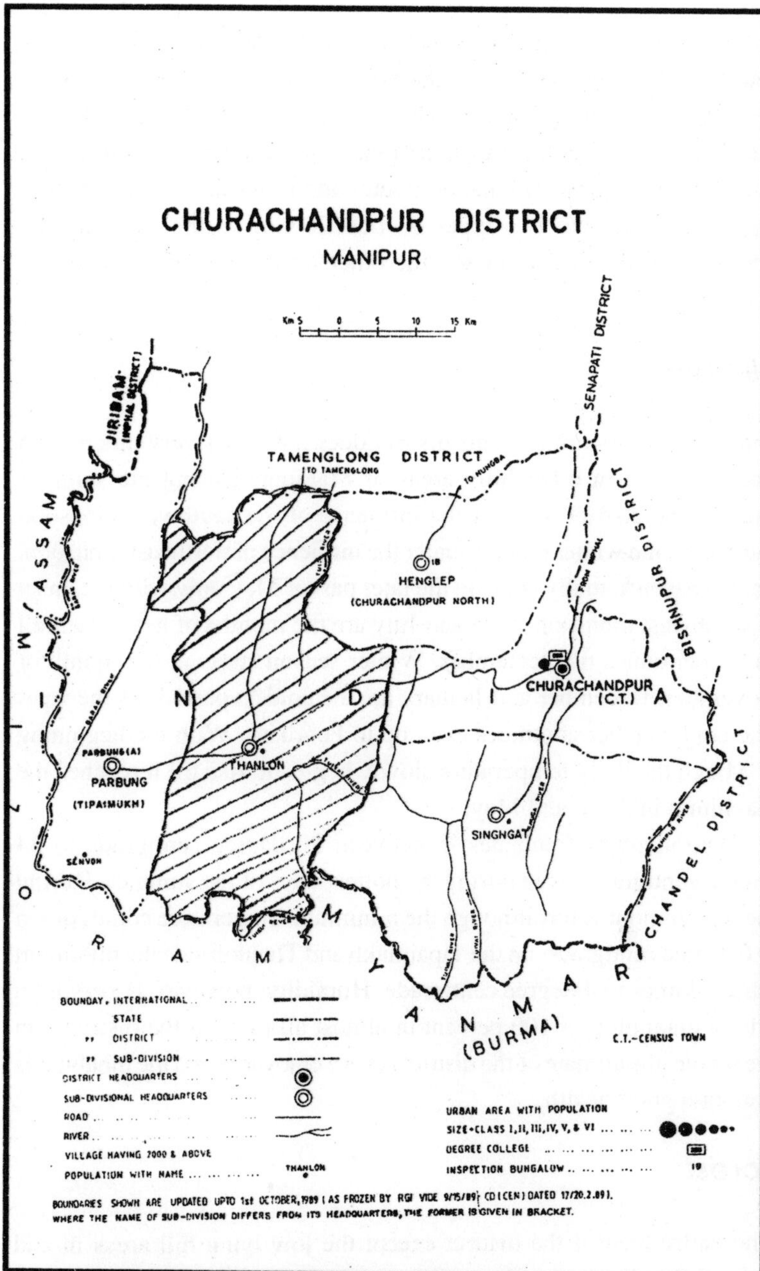

Map 4.2 : Map of Churachandpur District

and some portion of Thanlon and Singngat subdivision, and (3) the Southern hilly region covering the South East side of the District.

Many rivers and streams of which the most important are the Barak, the Manipur River, the Khuga, the Leimatak, and the Tuivai drain the district. The river system that originates and flows through the district can be grouped into two types — one flowing to the east into the Chindwin River in Burma and the other in the west into the Barak River.

Climate

The climate prevailing in this district does not differ very much from what is found in other hilly areas of Manipur. During the summer months, the district is under the influence of the southwest monsoon and during the winter months under the influence of northeast monsoon. Rainy season actually starts in the later part of May only with the onset of southwest monsoon. June and July are the months of heavy rainfall and it continues till September. Winter season starts in the month of November. December and January are the coldest periods of the year. The cold weather continues even up to February. With the beginning of March the daily temperature slowly begins to rise till it reaches the maximum in April and May.

The mercury fluctuates in between 30 degree centigrade to 34 degree centigrade, even during the hottest days of the summer. During the winter months too although the minimum temperature comes down to 0 degree centigrade, on the Tipaimukh and Thanlon side the minimum hardly comes to 4 degree centigrade. Humidity, however, is very high with a maximum of 100 percent in almost all parts of the district. On the whole, the climate of the district is very enjoyable and the inhabitants maintain good health.

Forest

The entire area of the district except the low lying hill areas in and around the district headquarters, is covered with forest of different varieties mostly of tropicai moist evergreen forest types. The hilly terrain nature, the rainfall and other climatic conditions prevailing in the district are conducive to a large and rich dense forests and bountiful natural vegetation. These dense forests support an abundant growth of many valuable trees, bamboo and grasses. These forests provide housing materials in the shape of timber, round wood, thatching grass, whole bamboo and bamboo splits for the mainframe, roofing and walls. The timbers, canes and bamboos are also very much in demand in furniture works. Other important forest products of the district are post and poles, charcoal, broom stick, *dalchini* and *uchithi* (a variety of species), cinnamon, *paateh/paasi* (local name of a variety of mushroom grown on old and worn trees), *gotuai thu* or *soibum* (local name of a product made from young bamboo shoot), smilex, honey, wax etc. These major and minor forest products are a constant source of considerable income to the meagre resource of the district. There are also a variety of forest products, which have medicinal properties besides the above-mentioned products.[3] (See appendix II for details). However in spite of the vast forest, resources available in all parts of the district nothing very tangible has been done to exploit it in a systematic manner. Whatever little had been exploited was done by the private entrepreneurs without any planning and proper consideration for an early recuperation of the forests in future. Jhuming cultivation, which involves burning down of vast forest areas, has also resulted in a large-scale destruction of the invaluable wealth besides affecting the ecological balance of the region.

Agriculture

Agriculture and the related activities provide the most dominant place in the economy of the district. Of the total workforce 80 percent are directly engaged in agricultural operations in 1991 of which cultivators account for 77 percent. Rice and maize are the most important agricultural products of the district.

Rice is cultivated on the slope of the hills through two methods, namely jhum and terrace cultivation. For the purpose of jhum, a plot of land is selected and the trees and the vegetation growing in it are slashed and cleared. Then fire is set and crops are finally sown on the clearing. Rain is the only source of water for such cultivation and production is low. The land thus brought under cultivation is used as long as it is fertile and productive. When the topsoil is finally washed away and the land becomes no longer productive, a fresh plot of land is selected for Jhuming. The jhum cycle or the rotation period is usually seven years but due to pressure on land increases, it has been gradually reduced to three or four years.

The terrace method of wet rice cultivation is generally practiced in areas where the inclinations of the hills are gradual and not very steep, particularly the foothills. This system of cultivation is almost the same as is done in the valley areas except that the enclosures in the hilly areas are usually very small. Spring and stream water are generally diverted for such purposes.

Besides rice and maize, the other important agricultural products of the district are pulses, potato, pea, soybeans, oil seeds, cotton, ginger, groundnut and chilies. Among vegetables mention may be made of cabbage, cauliflower, brinjal, tree bean *(yongchak* in local Manipuri language), tomatoes etc. A wide range of edible vegetables are also grown in the wild hills.

Minerals

The district is poor in mineral resources. No proper geological survey of all the areas of the district has been made till now. Only some deposits of lignite have been reported by the Geological Survey of India in and around Kangvai village in the Tureloo valley along the Tiddim State Highway. The total reserve of lignite in the area is estimated to be 12.262 tonnes. Presence of some precious stones are reported along the Myanmar (Burma) border.

Roads

The presence of a good means of road transport system is very essential for the overall economic development of a hilly district like Churachandpur. But because of terrain difficulties most of the villages of the district are very poorly connected with rest of the country. Even those roads, which are jeepable mostly in dry season, became very muddy and suffer from landslides during the rainy season.

PAITE'S : A BRIEF ACCOUNT OF THE STUDY TRIBE

The *Paites* are a tribe belonging to the Kuki-Chin-Mizo group of the Tibeto-Burman family. The *Paite* tribe mainly inhabit the hilly parts of Manipur and they are the fifth largest tribe in Manipur, out of the twenty-nine tribes recognized by the Government of India as Scheduled Tribes in Manipur.

The *Paites* were known by the term *'Kuki'* which was a nomenclature for the other twenty-eight tribes as well in Manipur, but the separate designation '*Paite*' came into existence in 1956-57 when the Government of India listed Scheduled Tribes, which also accorded separate terms to the other twenty-eight tribes as well. The name *paite*, comes from two words *pai* and *te* which refers to 'people moving towards different places' (Goswami and Kamkhenthang, 1972:21). The *Paites* inhabit mainly the Churachandpur district of Manipur. They speak *Paite* dialect, which belongs to the *Tibeto-Burman* family of *Kuki-Chin* group (Sen, 1992). They are a distinct tribe having their own customs and traditions and rules regarding succession, marriage, descent etc. The *Paite* according to their traditional story originated either in Tibet or in China from where they entered India *via* Burma. Their natural environment is hilly, mountainous, and referred to as Zougam. Its topography makes it unfit for wet cultivation or even terrace cultivation. They depend on the age-old system of *jhuming*. The *Paite* population of Manipur is 49,271 according to the census of 2001 (distributed over 125 villages and 5,078 households). Their language is *Paite*. It has many local variants. Sometimes the dialect is used to differentiate the various groups of *Paite*. For example, the *Paite* of Mizoram are known as *Dapzal* since a local dialect called *Dapzal* is used by them, which has, many words borrowed from the *Lushai* language.

Serological studies reveal a high frequency of blood group A (35.37 percent) closely followed by blood group B (31.09 percent). Similarly a high percentage of the R'R" gene (72.05%) has been found in the blood group RH of this community. They eat the flesh of all animals except the snakes, carnivores and birds. Their staple food is rice. Formally, this used to be maize supplemented job's tears, millet, sulphur bean, corn, sweet potato, etc. (Encyclopaedia of Manipur, 2001).

However, now these are not taken regularly since rice is available through fair-price shops. Vegetables cultivated in jhum fields are creeper beans of various types, snake-gourd, brinjal, mustard, pumpkins, ginger, chili, and spices. Besides, cucumber, melon, watermelon are also grown on the same plot of land. The most important drink available was beer prepared indigenously from rice, job's tears and millet. This was offered to the Gods, evil spirit as well as friends and visitor. It was consumed amid festivities on ritual occasions.

Milk was not taken in past. After conversion to Christianity the church dissuaded people from drinking rice-beer since a large quantity of precious foodstuff was consumed in the process of brewing this alcoholic liquor. Due to negligible yield of paddy and maize from jhum cultivation the community went hungry almost three months in a year. Therefore, tea was introduced as a social drink in place of *Zu* (rice-beer). Tea with or without milk is now as common as rice-beer was in the past. Offering a rice-beer to relatives such as the mother's brother and as a gift for marriage negotiation, etc., has been replaced by offering of tea. Formally every household brewed rice-beer. This practice is still prevalent among non-Christians. The *Paites* also depend so much on their indigenous medicinal substances for their minor health problems. Every *Paite* village used to have traditional healers whom they referred to as *'siampu'*. The rich natural resources of their region make them rich in indigenous medicinal knowledge. They used to survive major and minor illnesses by using indigenous treatment. It is a very recent phenomenon that they started approaching allopath doctors with the change in their socio-economic conditions. The kind of medicinal substances that are still prevalent among the *Paites* are given in the appendices.

Cultural practices of Paite tribe

The *Paite* tribe has undergone what Srinivas had term as "westernization" which is defined by him as change brought about in Indian society and culture as a result of British rule. The coming of the British especially to the evolvement of what the *Paite* tribes are today.

The *Paite* tribes are a tribe in transition. They embody both traditional values and modern values. They retain traditional customs like appointing *Inndongta* (household council), which is essential for a married couple after having a separate house to have a household council. This household council takes up matters like death, loss, marriage or any other celebrations in the house etc. The household council should consist of the following members :

(1) INTEK — The Householder

(2) THALLOUH — A closely related brother who may be dear to the householder is appointed as *'thallouh'*

(3) THUSAPI — A reliable person from other clan who can help the household in terms of advice or suggestion in times of trouble, is generally appointed as THUSAPI (first), others *'thusa'* may be appointed as and when necessary like: THUSA NIHNA (second) and THUSA THUMNA (third)

(4) TANUPI — Householder elder sister is appointed as TANUPI
TANU NIHNA — Householder second sister, if any
TANU THUMNA — Householder third sister, if any

(5) PUPI — Mother's brother of householder is called *'pupi'*

(6) PUNAU — The wife's brother or in-laws of householder is called *'punau'*

(7) BEHVAL — The fourth 'thusa' having no specific assignment in the distribution of work is called *'behval'*

(8) ZAWL — A friend of householder but of other clan is appointed as *'zawl'*

The *Paites* also retain the following traditional customs or cultural practices:

TOU SAGOH: It is a feast arranged by a married younger brother by killing a four-footed animal to the house of the eldest brother as a token of respect to his eldest brother and a symbol of making an independent household on the part of the younger brother. When such feast is arranged, the eldest brother gives certain properties to the younger brother to start an independent life. If a younger brother does not arrange such a feast then it is presumed that it is disrespect towards his brother. But no fine is imposed for not performing such TOUSA.

PUZUKHOLH: A nephew pays respect to his maternal uncle by bringing ZU (rice beer but now replaced by tea) as a token of love and respect, the latter gives blessing to his nephew and organizes a feast in honour of his nephew.

MINPHUAH (naming a child): When a child is born to a married couple, if it is a boy it is given name by the child's grandfather or any male member of the child's father. Taking the last syllable of the person's name that is naming the child does the naming. Likewise if the child is a girl, the grandmother of the child or any female member of the father or mother's side will give name to the child.

KITENNA (marriage): In regard to marriage, the boy's family with their household council members, go to the girl's family with a kettle of tea, and asked for the girl's hand. If there is no breach of engagement between a boy or a girl till the date fixed for marriage, a marriage ceremony is performed with the knowledge of the household council, which consists of family members, relatives and close friends and also with the knowledge of the public in the church, and after then, the boy and girl become husband and wife. The bridegroom has to pay a bride price to the bride's parents. Earlier they used to pay in kind—three *mithuns* of which one is female and the calf must be included, also in coins where the coins would be kept in *'lawhpi'* or traditional basket and brought to the bride's family.

The *Paite* tribe follows a patrilineal descent line. The male is the head of the family, a woman moves out at the time of her marriage, and children born belong to the husband family. The eldest son is entitled to succeed to the properties of his father at the time of his death; but the father has got the right to divide or distribute his properties to the other sons before he dies. In case, the head of the family dies without making distribution of his properties to his children, then the household council in the presence of the children can make distribution of properties to the children of the deceased father. If the head of the family has no son of his own at the time of his death to succeed or inherit his properties both movable and immovable, then the properties will go to the nearest male member of his relatives or to his next brother.

The *Paite* tribe also follows a practice of what is called 'patriliteral cross cousin's marriage' which the *Paite* refers to as *'ni nungzui'*, which when translated means following the father's sister. It means that a girl can get married to her father's sister's son.

The *Paite* tribe has many clans. These clans can trace their descent up to the forefathers. Inter-marriage of clans is allowed; marriage within one clan is also allowed, i.e. intra-marriage of clans (Jamkhanthang & Thangchinlian, 1986).

Social organization of Paite tribe

Paite tribes are in majority among other tribes who inhabit Churachandpur district. Each tribe has a distinct social order as well as community laws. Let us see in brief the social organization of the *'Paite'* in particular.

The system of hereditary chiefship as well as community ownership of village land is prevalent among the *Paite* tribe. In case of hereditary chiefship the chief is all-powerful, as he controls not only the village economy through his ownership of land but exercises social control over the households in the village. From minor case to criminal cases like murder etc. are decided by him with the help of the "*upa's*"(elders). In regard to distribution of jhum land, the chief, his *upa's* and the village crier, just select jhum lands and then the general public follow suit. The chief also has the privileged of receiving various taxes from the villagers like:

(1) PADDY TAX (BUHSUN): It is the duty of every household

in the village to pay at least a tax of one basket of rice per annum for use by the chief's household, the tax usually varied.

(2) MEAT TAX (SALIANG): Whenever a villager kill a four footed wild animal, a portion of the meat was paid to the chief as tax.

(3) BEE TAX (KHUAI SIAH): If a villager extracted honey, the chief was paid his share, being the owner of the land.

Although the chief enjoyed enormous powers, these are not without limitations. If the chief became tyrannical, indifferent to the welfare of his subjects, or inefficient in tackling the administration, the villagers could desert him at any time.

The *Paite* tribe follows a patriarchal society. The women are not discriminated against anything. They play a significant role in agriculture, animal husbandry, besides being actively involved in weaving.

An overwhelming majority (almost all) of the *Paite* population has converted to Christianity. Christianity has not materially changed the social order but was the critical faith in bringing to an end the head hunting wars and savagery that characterized early tribal societies. Christianity has a far-reaching influence on the *Paite* tribe. Community festivals and taboos and ceremonies were replaced by Christian festivals such as New Year's Day, Christmas, Good Friday, Easter Sunday etc. There is total disappearance of animal sacrifices, which used to consume a considerable portion of all the earnings of the tribal people. Christianity has completely changed their social life and modifies some of their cultural practices.

Even the education that took place through the Missionaries established schools and learning centres has helped the *Paites* to be polished in their ways of life. The *Paite* society is more or less an egalitarian society, there exists no caste system. There is not much of a rich or poor divide.

The recognition by the Government of India as one of the Scheduled Tribes of India, entitles the *Paite* of protection and of their progress and development and well-being. The *Paites* have established themselves as a distinct tribe having their own customs and traditions.

The *Paite* tribe during the past had to a large extent the characteristics of mechanical solidarity. Here by mechanical solidarity, Durkheim meant to say that there is a strong system of social links between the individual and society based on obligation, custom and sentiment. Collective rules and social practices are predominantly religious in nature and a strong common conscience pervades all aspects of social life.

However, the social organization started changing. Now, at present, mechanical solidarity has given way to organic solidarity. Here, again Durkheim meant by organic solidarity is those occupational functions becoming more specialized. There is a larger population spread over broader geographic areas. Likewise, the *Paite* tribe in present time are showing some characteristics of organic solidarity. The individual no longer is very much bounded by village rules or religious beliefs. He has started up his own nuclear family network. He starts gaining specialization in various fields. A shift from the traditional occupation of cultivation and farming to white collar jobs become popular (Guite, 1999; Durkheim, 1961).

THE STUDY VILLAGES

Thanlon subdivision of Churachandpur district is one of the most backward subdivisions of the district. Thanlon is the subdivisional headquarters of the subdivision and is situated on the Churachandpur-Tipaimukh Road (Map 4.3).

The subdivision is bounded on the north by Tamenglong district; on the east by Churachandpur north subdivision, Churachandpur and Singngat subdivision; on the west by Tipaimukh subdivision and on the south by Mizoram and Myanmar. This subdivision has no water supply for its forty-seven villages. It lacks very much in terms of communication and educational institution. The majority of the people belong to the *Paite* tribe. The subdivision have no hospital and has to depend on the district hospital located in the district headquarters. Out of the forty-seven villages in the subdivision, only fifteen villages have medical facilities in the form of dispensary, primary health

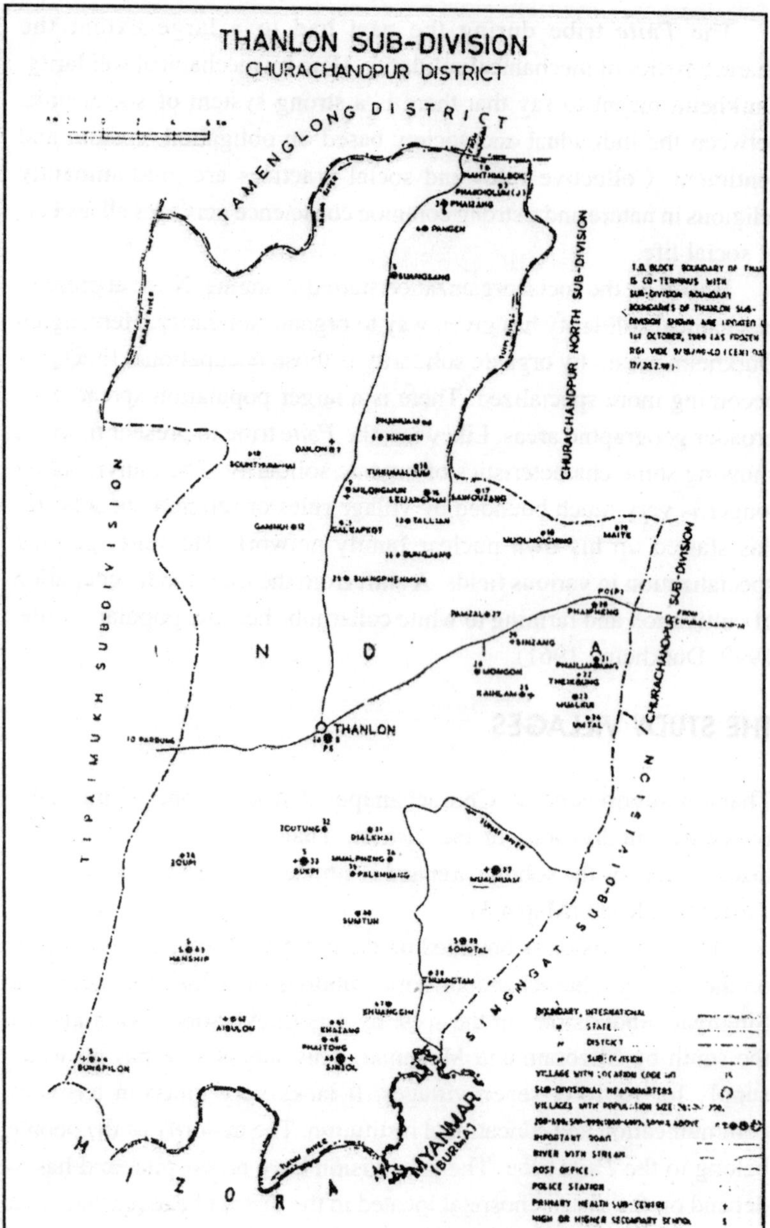

Map 4.3 : Map of Thanlon Subdivision

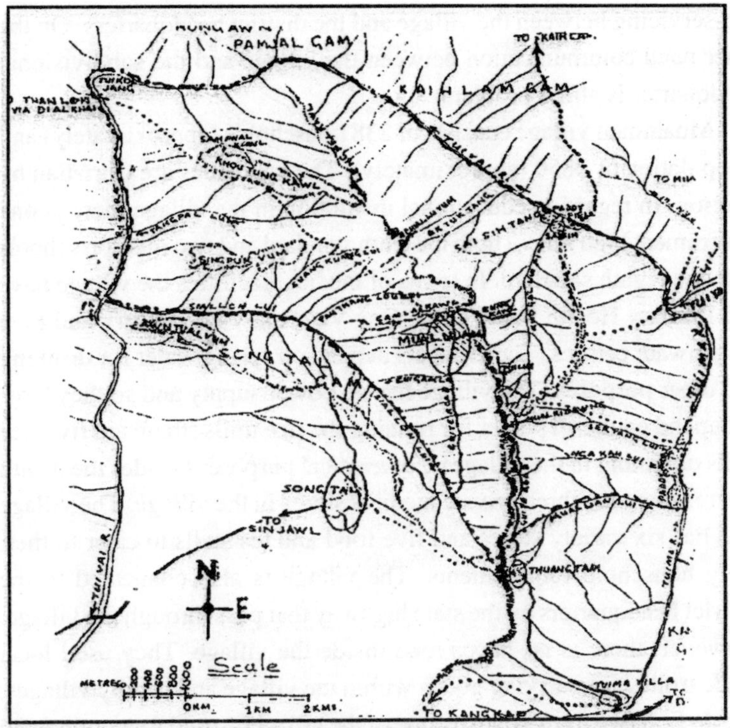

Fig. 4.1 : Topography of Mualnuam and Thuangtam Villages

centre and primary health centre. Both the study villages—Mualnuam and Thuangtam falls under Thanlon sub division and located on the southeastern side of Thanlon (Map 4.4 and Map 4.5).

Profile of Mualnuam and Thuangtam village

Mualnuam is a very old village, older than the district headquarter. The forefather of the *Paites* settled here and spread out slowly in search of a more fertile and suitable place to settle. The village is 130 km far from the district headquarter. There was no road communicating the village with the district and also with the sub-divisional headquarter till the nineties. Even now roads are rough and barren. During the dry season it is dusty while it is muddy and landslides prone during the rainy season. Due to such situation, hardly two or three buses are found sub-servicing between the village and the district headquarters. On the other hand communication between the village and the subdivisional headquarter is still a problem.

Mualnuam village consists of 238 households (approximately) and a population of 1850 (approximately). The majorities are Christian by religion. In regard to educational institution in the village there is one government high school upto the tenth standard and two mission schools upto the eighth standard. In terms of medical facilities the village have one Primary Health Sub-Centre, One Veterinary Dispensary and Five Anganwadi centres. The villagers depend on spring water for drinking and other purposes. The village has no power supply and so they have to depend on diesel power for running the rice mills (there are five rice mills operating in the village). For medical purposes besides the health centres there are three private medical stores in the village. The village also has six variety stores and five food and tea stalls to cater to their daily household requirements. The village is also connected to the district headquarters by the state highway that pass through the village. However, there is no *pucca* road inside the village. They used local made trolley for carrying goods within the village and nearby villages. We do find two trucks own by one of the villagers, used for commercial purposes. We can see shift in occupation of the villagers but as a whole their main occupation is agriculture where they practice both Jhum and terrace cultivation.

Thuangtam is a very small village with a population of around 420 and 70 households. Paite tribe is in majority and in fact there is no other tribe in the village. It is 110 kilometres far from the district headquarters. Thuangtam comes before Mualnuam if we come by road from the district headquarters. The state highway that comes from the district headquarters passes through Singngat subdivision and then comes into Thanlon subdivision. The highway then passes through both village A and B and then to Mizoram. The roads are rough and barren during dry season. It is muddy and landslides occur during rainy season.

As compared to Mualnuam village, it is far less develop. The basic amenities are absent in the village. There is a distance of 20 km between

Mualnuam and Thuangtam village. So in any emergency situation villagers of Thuangtam village run to Mualnuam village. The majority of this village are also Christians by religion and *Paite* dominated village. As mentioned earlier there are no proper basic amenities in regard to educational institution, medical facilities and power supply. They depend on the rice mill of Mualnuam village in emergency otherwise they used traditional method. For their daily requirements, they have one medical store, variety store and food/tea stall. They are also depending on the spring water for drinking and other purposes. They have to go quite a distance to fetch water unlike Mualnuam village that connected water pipes inside the village. Only local made trolleys are found in the village for carrying goods. Their main occupation is agriculture both jhum and terrace cultivation.

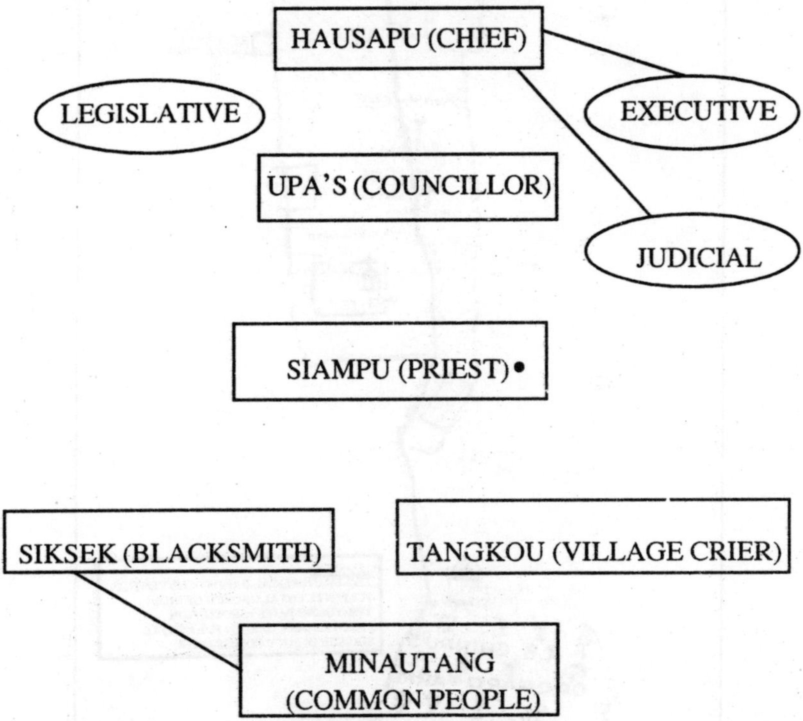

- Now replace by PASTOR/ ELDERS of the Church
- Now replace by village authority

Fig 4.2 : Village Structure

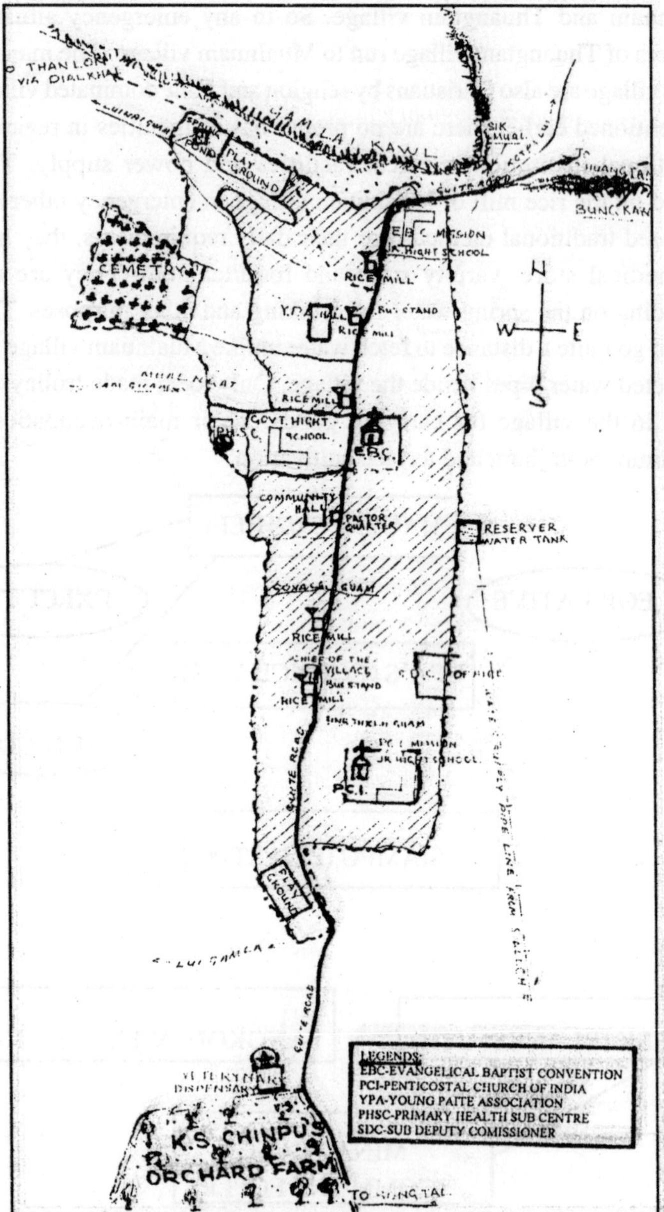

Map 4.4 : Map of Mualnuam village

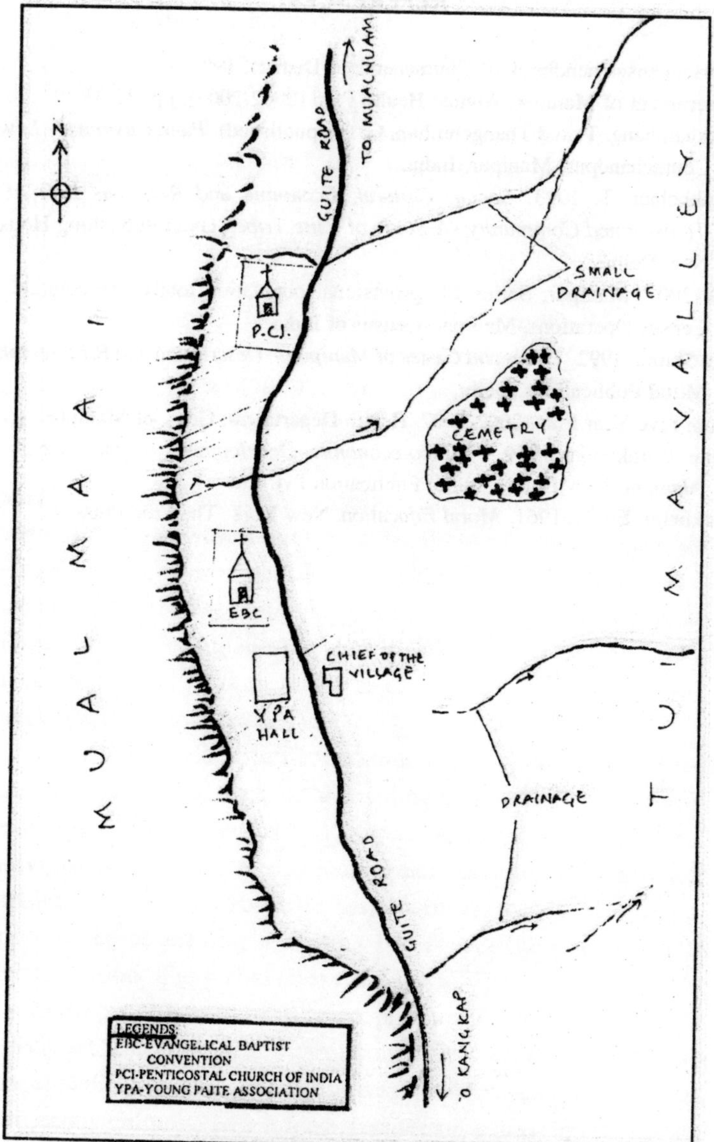

Map 4.5 : Map of Thuangtam village

REFERENCES

District census handbook of Churachandpur District, 1991.

Government of Manipur, Annual Health Plan (2002-2003); pp. 32-33.

Jamkhanthang, T. and Thangchinlian, G. (Unpublished). *Paite Customary Laws*, Churachandpur, Manipur, India.

Liankhohau, T. 1993. *Social, Cultural, Economic and Religious Life of a Transformed Community (A Study of Paite Tribe)*, Gyan Publishing House, New Delhi.

RGI 2001. Manipur, Series 14 (provisional population totals), Directorate of Census Operations, Manipur, Census of India.

Sen, Shipra. 1992. *Tribes and Castes of Manipur—Description and Bibliography*, Mittal Publications, Delhi.

Tenth Five Year Plan, 2002-2007. Health Department, Govt. of Manipur.

Guite Chinkholian.1999. *Politico-economic Development of the Tribals of Manipur*, New Delhi: Anmol Publication Pvt. Ltd.

Durkheim, Emile. 1961. *Moral Education*, New York: The Free Press.

5

Health, Disease and Care Utilisation

In this chapter the socio-demographic composition, economic status, perception of diseases, their belief system and case studies of traditional healer and para-medic health personnel of both the study villages will be discussed and presented using tables and figures.

PROFILE OF THE STUDY POPULATION

(1) Age Composition

The age composition of the two villages reflects that Mualnuam is 'younger' than Thuangtam (Table 5.1). The age composition of the respondents suggests that almost half of the respondents in Thuangtam are in the working/reproductive ages and almost one-third in both the villages are aged 45 and above. As regards the respondents aged below 24 years, most of them (30%) are in Mualnuam than Thuangtam (20%). Age composition of the sample population suggests close similarities between the two villages. While the adolescent population in almost same, Mualnuam with 33.3 per cent, less than 15 years as compared to 32 per cent in Thuangtam, the working age group population is more in Thuangtam (59%) as compared to Mualnuam (57%). The share of 'an old adult (46-60 years) is also more in Thuangtam (18%) than in Mualnuam

(13.3%). However, the elderly (60+) are more in Mualnuam (11.1%) as compared to Thuangtam (8.3%).

Table 5.1 : Age Composition

Thuangtam % Persons	*Age Group*	*Mualnuam % Persons*
Respondent		*Respondent*
20	Below 24	30
50	24-44	40
30	45 and above	30
Sample Population		*Sample Population*
31.67	Below 15	33.3
20.0	16-30	22.2
21.67	31-45	20.0
18.35	46-60	13.3
8.34	60 and above	11.1

Source: Field Survey 2003.

Most elderly stay at home and take care of the grandchildren or make *'lenkha zial'* local cigarettes.

(2) Education

As regards to educational level, Mualnuam appears to be more literate than Thuangtam. While in Mualnuam 30 per cent of respondents and 11 per cent of family members are illiterate, in the other village 68 per cent respondents and 55 per cent family members are illiterate. Half of the respondents in Mualnuam as compared to 32 per cent in Thuangtam have attained primary level education. In Mualnuam 16 per cent respondents and 27 per cent family members have studied upto high school. It is interesting to note that 4 per cent respondents in Mualnuam and only 0.03 per cent family members in Thuangtam have studied graduation. In Thuangtam village there is no educational institution. So there are more illiterate population than literate ones (Table 5.2).

Table 5.2 : Education Attainment

Village/persons	*Illiterate*	*Primary*	*High School*	*Graduate*
Mualnuam				
Respondent	30.0	50.0	16.0	04.0
Sample Population	11.1	61.1	26.6	—
Thuangtam				
Respondent	68	32.0	—	—
Sample Population	55.0	40.0	4.7	0.3

Source: Field Survey 2003.

In Mualnuam village the females are generally married early as they attain puberty. Educating the females is not given much priority and therefore, they themselves also do not have much interest in education. Some of them also work as an agent of anganwadi centre that they open in their respective houses under the ICDS programme of the Central Government. Fifty per cent of the respondents who did till primary have just enough knowledge to read and write their own dialect (Paite's script is Roman script). The two graduates among the respondents are school teachers in the mission school.

In Thuangtam village there used to be a high school but it was shut down as there is no regular student. So due to poor performance the State government re-locate the school to some other village.

(3) Family Structure

It is a patriarchal society in both the villages. Generally, the parents stay with the eldest son. There is both nuclear and joint family. In Mualnuam village, 70 per cent are nuclear family and 30 per cent are joint family. While in Thuangtam village 60 per cent are in nuclear family and the rest 40 per cent are in joint family. Thus, nuclearisation of family is more in Mualnuam than Thuangtam.

(4) Land Holding Pattern

Both the study villages have the same land holding pattern. Village land belongs to the Chief. Villagers can have houses and practice *jhum* cultivation on it. Chief with the help of his Councillors (Upa's) and village authority, set apart every year certain portion of the land for *jhuming*. Chief, his councilors and village authority, just select *jhum* lands and then the general public follow suits through ticket system. Terrace cultivation at the foothills of the village is also done with the permission the Chief of the village.

(5) Housing pattern, assets and livestock

In Mualnuam village, 66.3 per cent of the respondents are living in *kuccha* houses (house with thatched roof or bamboo walls and floors), and 33.7 per cent are living in *pucca* houses (house with tin roof and wooden walls and floors). Electric power supply do not reach both the villages. Assets possessed by the respondents excluding others, mention may be made of radio (listened by using battery), and two respondents have one truck each for business purpose, five rice mills in the village run by diesel generator. In Thuangtam village, 80 per cent of the respondents are living in *kuccha* houses and the rest 20 per cent in *pucca* houses. Radio is the only media that links them to outside world. There is only one rice mill in the village. In both the villages, livestock comprises cow, pig, goat, and horse, which serve their daily purposes whether it be for milk, oil, meat, ploughing and as a goods carrier or even as a source of income. Thus, Mualnuam appears to be more prosperous than Thuangtam. However, the overall economic status of the respondents from both the villages is low. They produce just enough for their own consumption and sometimes not even enough to last for one whole year. It is a patriarchal society but the women play a significant role in agriculture and animal husbandry, besides being actively involved in weaving (Table 5.3).

Table 5.3 : Quality of Life

Quality of life	*Mualnuam*	*Thuangtam*
Kuccha houses	66	80
Pucca houses	34	20
Electricity	—	—
Radio	Yes	Yes
Truck	(2) Yes	—
Rice Mills	(5) Yes, diesel operated	(1)

Source: Field Survey 2003.

Generally the villages have a low socio-economic status. There are resources but no proper infrastructure to develop the natural resources for the economic benefits of the people. They produce and cultivate just enough for their own consumption and sometimes not even enough for themselves depending on the climatic conditions. It is a patriarchal society but the women do play a significant role in agriculture, animal husbandry, weaving besides being consulted in household decision making.

PERCEPTION OF DISEASE CAUSATION

Perception of disease causation included unhealthy food habits, poor diet, ignorance and lack of awareness; beliefs relating causation with evil spirit; unsafe drinking water and sanitation; and poverty as a sign of economic insufficiency causing depression, loss of appetite leading to ill health. About 26.4 per cent of the respondents mention poverty as one of the main cause of disease, due to which they are unable to afford good diet, work harder in the field and sometimes have to spend the night in the field that exposed them to diseases like malaria. The other contributory causes of diseases mention are unhealthy food habits (20%), ignorance about preventive measures (18%), poor diet (12%), beliefs that disease are caused by evil spirit (5.8%), unsafe drinking water (12%), poor sanitation (5.8%) like *kuccha*/open latrine that provides a breading grounds for mosquitoes spreading malaria in the village.

PATTERN OF DISEASES

The disease pattern can be divided as major and minor illnesses. Children are more prone to illnesses, which are seasonal and minor in nature. The women complain of reproductive health problems like constant white discharge, urinary tract infection, anemia, complication related to pregnancy. The men folk are more prone to malaria and tuberculosis. Their occupation demands them to stay back in the field for days or three since the distance between village and field is not feasible to communicate back and forth. There are also cases of mental illnesses, fits, epilepsy and polio in the villages. There is no much difference of disease pattern in both villages. It may be due to close proximity, same cultural practices, same occupation, similar food habits and settlement patterns.

UTILIZATION PATTERN OF DIFFERENT SYSTEMS OF MEDICINE

Indigenous medicinal substances are usually utilized for minor illnesses. In Mualnuam village, 60 per cent (30 out of 50 respondents) prefer to use indigenous medicinal substances for minor illnesses while 56 per cent (28 out of 50 respondents) go to hospital (allopathic medicine) for major illnesses. 10 per cent and 6 per cent of them do not seek any treatment in minor illnesses and major illnesses respectively. The reasons are most of the times due to financial difficulties and sometimes where they feel that there is no hope. On the other hand, the dependence on indigenous medicinal substances is high in Thuangtam village due to the absence of proper medical facilities. 80 per cent and 30 per cent of them utilized indigenous medicine for minor and major illnesses respectively. No primary health centre is located in the village and therefore, they approach the only medical store both in minor and major illnesses. 6 per cent resort to no treatment at all. There is little awareness about Indian system of medicine (Ayurveda, Homoeopathy, Unani, Siddha) and thus there is no question of utilizing it.

In terms of preference for treatment majority of them preferred hospital (also means better facilities) for both minor and major illnesses. The primary health subcentre in Mualnuam village gets no preference as it is not functioning properly. Here the medical store is popular and it keeps the basic for first aid and pain relief.

BELIEF SYSTEM OF THE RESPONDENTS

Belief in the Allopathic and indigenous system of medicine exists together. However dependence on allopathic is much higher as compared to other system as it is the official medicine of the government. However in regard to psychological illnesses belie in allopathic treatment is hardly visible. They generally feel that there is no treatment for mental illnesses. In the past the respondents used to approach the traditional healer or the priest (*siampu*) with the belief in his spiritual and magical power. Conversion to Christianity stopped all there practices of animal sacrifices to please the spirits for curing a sick person. So usually no treatment is done but they requested the pastors or the elders of the church to pray for the patients keeping the faith that it will heal.

The belief system is more or less the same in both the villages. There is in fact no difference to mention. Religion plays an important role in changing their perception towards health, medicines and also their entire outlook towards life.

Regarding the role of a traditional healer, both the study villages feel that the role has undergone changes. They no longer practice as they feel inferior as compared to other system of medicine. The knowledge on indigenous medicinal substances now becomes an alternative and as home remedy. There is no attempt or effort on the part of the villagers to promote and protect the knowledge on medicinal substances as they were not aware about the value and vulnerability of their knowledge in the light of the changes brought about by the new economic policy after the 1990s. They have accepted the change brought about by the larger socio-economic milieu.

CASE STUDIES

Traditional Healers/Folk Practitioners

According to the definition of the World Health Organization (WHO), 'a traditional healer is a person who is recognized by the community in which he lives as competent to provide health care by using vegetable, animal and mineral substances and certain other methods based on the social, cultural and religious background as well as on the knowledge and attitude and beliefs that are prevalent in the community regarding physical, mental and social well-being and the causation of disease and disability.'

As defined by WHO, there used to be a traditional healer each in both the study villages. The traditional healer of Thuangtam village has just passed away sometimes ago, so the account of traditional healer from this village cannot be gathered. In Mualnuam village the traditional healer was available though he was not practicing any more. An abstract of interview with him is given below.

Profile

The traditional healer, age 70, was educated up to primary level. In his family there were two male and four female members. His wife was illiterate, have two sons and three daughters. They have education up to primary and high school. The family cultivated on *jhum* land given by the Chief. He seems to have lost his social status as traditional healer, which he enjoyed in the past. It may be probably he stopped practicing. He lives in a *pucca* house with tin roof and wooden floor with his family forming a joint family. He possesses a radio and a trolley, which is used for carrying goods from market to his house. His livestock comprises horse, buffalo and some poultry.

Professional History

He practiced for thirty years. He got into the profession through his uncle (father's younger brother). His uncle was a fourth grade employee under Mizoram Government but he left that job, came back to his village and started his practice. He developed his interest and skills by observing his uncle's practice. Then he became a full time practioner. He was called '*siampu*' (priest) during those times.

According to him, the kind of diseases healed constitutes from minor to major illnesses and mental illnesses too. The diseases were :

- Stomache, fever, headache, fits (*phungjawl*);
- Mental illnesses which he term it as '*dawimat*' which means possessed by evil spirit, Jaundice which he terms it as '*mit-eng*' (yellow eyes);
- Muscle and nerves problem in the whole body especially of the legs and hands, which is called '*thaguina, khekham, khutkham*' in Paite dialect;
- Skin related problems; and
- Lastly, he also treated a kind of polio cases which they called as '*kumzawn*' in Paite dialect.

The kind of medicinal substances used for treatment were from plants, herbs, tubers, water and animal species. He also has the special book that contains specific words and sentences to be uttered while giving treatment. He made an idol using mud and worships that idol by offering animal sacrifices every time before he started his practice. He generally used dog, goat, hen among the animals. For treating fits he remembers mixing grinded prone or crab and blood of any animal, gave it to the idol and to the patients after performing and uttering the necessary rituals.

There are many more interesting incidents that he said that he couldn't recollect it accurately. It was ten years, i.e. a decade or so that he had stopped practicing. Quoting him, he said, 'I'm the last traditional healer and it is my duty to hand it over to my children or to anyone but everyone stop believing in this practice. I, myself also stop believing now because I have become a Christian, a religion which showed me the path of truth, which over power the devil and freed me from the bondage of evil spirit.'

However he strongly recommends using medicinal substances for health care needs but not in the way he practiced. He feels that he is using a kind of witch craft which people cannot accept. He also asserted that as medicinal plants grow in the wild forests, cultivation of it may not be a very good proposal until it offers health and economic benefits to the people. At the same time he feels that some of the medicinal plants which he used were on the verge of extinction and needs to be preserved. With the increase in population, the practice of *jhum* cultivation created an ecological imbalance. The medicinal substances become rare and inaccessible.

In the past, during his prime time of practicing, he was given a respectable position in the village. He used to carry out death ceremony and also have full authority in punishing a criminal. He does receive gifts in the form of traditional clothes, a basket of paddy etc. He perceives his social status as very high.

Interview with the Para-Medical Staff of Mualnuam Village

The health service system in the whole district of Churachandpur is very poor. Lack of infrastructure, irresponsible health personnel, and political instability etc. characterizes the district health service scenario. Besides this, the rural health services is nil with no proper infrastructure but the health employees were prompt in collecting their unearned salary.

In Mualnuam village there is one primary health sub-centre but not so in Thuangtam village. The researcher could not locate the Para-medical staff working in the health centre of Mualnuam village residing within the village itself. On the other hand a respondent was required from the health personnel side. So after many enquiries, she could locate one of the employee of Mualnuam Village PHC in the district headquarters. He is the compounder (pharmacist by qualification) of the health centre. There are besides him three other fourth grade employees.

An abstract of the interview with him is given below:

He is in Mualnuam PHSC since March 1985. According to him, the villagers utilized the services of the PHSC in the beginning. The approximate percentage of the population using the services are around 80 per cent. There were good responses towards his prescribed treatment. Severe illnesses that needed hospitalization were usually referred to district hospital in the district headquarters.

The attitude of the people towards PHSC started changing after no medicines were available free. He feels that otherwise the people had given good response towards the national health programes like family planning programme, immunization programme, malaria control programme etc. that are still continuing when the funds come from the state capital. He very much appreciates the Central Government approach on the national health programmes and its aim to secure health for all at a minimum cost for the people. At the same time he is disappointed to see that none of the funds allocated were utilized, as it should be. He defended his failure to provide services to the villagers by blaming it on the lack of infrastructure. He said that he cannot stay in the village with his family because of no proper school for his children and no accommodation provided by the government.

He, however, recommended the use of indigenous medicinal substances "cent-per-cent". He narrated his experience during his training, as a pharmacist where he found that the ingredients contained in allopathic medicine is more or less the same with what the ingredients of indigenous medicine. He feels that given the scenario of the district health service system, it is very important to revive our use and faith in traditional medicine so that this can at least meet the basic health care needs of the people.

Lastly, on the question of the kind of problem he faced while performing and rendering his duties, he said that he could not perform his duties without medicine, other staff, and basic facilities like beds and other required materials. Ironically speaking, only PHSC building is there to be seen and that is why he is with his family in the district headquarters.

6

Summary and Conclusions

SUMMARY

The Alma Ata Declaration of 1978 to attain 'Health For All' through Primary Health Care (PHC) approach was applauded the world-over. This brought the issue of improving and strengthening the public health infrastructure in all the signatory countries including India. The government as a result, has been concentrating on the development of rural health infrastructure so as to provide curative, promotive and preventive health services to 74.3 percentage of our rural population through Community Health Centres (CHCs), Primary Health Centres (PHCs) and Health Sub-Centres (SCs).

This study, attempts to examine the utilization pattern of indigenous medicinal substances by rural population and identify the various factor that impede their use. The study was undertaken to capture the dynamics of the interaction and changes that have occurred in relations to utilization of indigenous medicinal substances and folk practitioners. The study explored the changes in folk medicine with introduction of allopathy, how these changes in structure of provisioning had influenced the health seeking behaviour of the community. Thus the main focus of the study was to locate and capture the changes in health seeking behaviour of the people within the overall socio-economic milieu.

For the purpose of this study, the 'Paites' of Churachandpur district from Manipur was seiected as they are the majority tribe in the district, and can be a representative of the other smaller tribes living in the district. Out of the 47 villages in Thanlon sub-division of Churachandpur district, two villages, namely Mualnuam and Thuangtam were selected purposively on the basis of basic amenities available and found in the villages. This study was conducted over a period of two months of intense fieldwork of a participatory nature. The study had both a quantitative and qualitative dimensions to it. The quantitative dimensions tried to elicit broadly the socio-economic features and health seeking behaviour of the population in the two study villages. In each of the village roughly fifty households ware selected on the basis of housing structure as this indicates the socio-economic status in both the villages. This provided a macro picture of the villager's socio-economic conditions. This was substantiated with in-depth case studies and profiles of folk practitioners. For the community, in-depth interviews were used to get some qualitative insights into their perceptions and behaviour.

INDIGENOUS SYSTEM OF MEDICINE

Approach and emerging issues

The prevailing health and medical system, the Western system, has unfortunately failed to meet the need of the world's majority. The failure of the Alma Ata Declaration in fulfilling its objectives of achieving Health for all by the year 2000 gives more urgency for looking at an approach that is alternative of the existing medical system. The government, which provided medicines free of cost to the PHCs, could not satisfy the growing demand for these drugs with its budget constraints and allocation to other aspects of health. Today there are no drugs available in several PHCs set up by the government, a very good example being the study villages themselves.

Also with the advent of the New Economic Policy in 1991, the World Bank and International Monetary Fund give less and less emphasis to the social and welfare sectors and higher emphasis to the economic and infrastructure sectors. The implication of such a trend in countries, where health insurance is unaffordable to the majority, is unimaginable. Another issue of importance is that due to the influence of new wonder drugs, their heavy advertising and commercialization, people's faith in low cost traditional medicines has decreased. Based on current trends in health care financing and failure of the Alma Ata Declaration to take grip of the situation, there is an imperative need for evolving an *Alternative*. In this whole situation, the condition of the poor, particularly the indigenous people have become more critical and difficult.

THE RURAL PRIMARY HEALTH CARE SYSTEM

The institutional structure

The Primary Health Delivery System is a three-tier hierarchical institutional structure.

> *Sub-Centre*—It is the first contact point between the primary health care system and the community, manned by one multipurpose male worker and one multipurpose female worker (who generally is auxiliary nurse midwife—ANM). The SC is in-charge of the promotive and preventive activities within a group of villages. The *anganwadi* worker (AWW) and trained birth attendants (TBA) at the village level provide support to SC.
>
> *Primarey Health Centre*— It is the first contact point between the village community and the Medical Officer (MO). A PHC acts as a referral unit for six subcentres. The activities of PHC involve curative, preventive, promotive and family welfare services. Fourteen paramedical and other staff manned it.
>
> *Community Health Centre* — It serves as a referral centre for four PHCs. Its staff consists of four medical specialists, supported by 21 paramedical and other staff.

Since the unit of analysis is the PHC and the area covered by it, the staffing pattern of only the PHC and the SC have been represented in Figure 6.1.

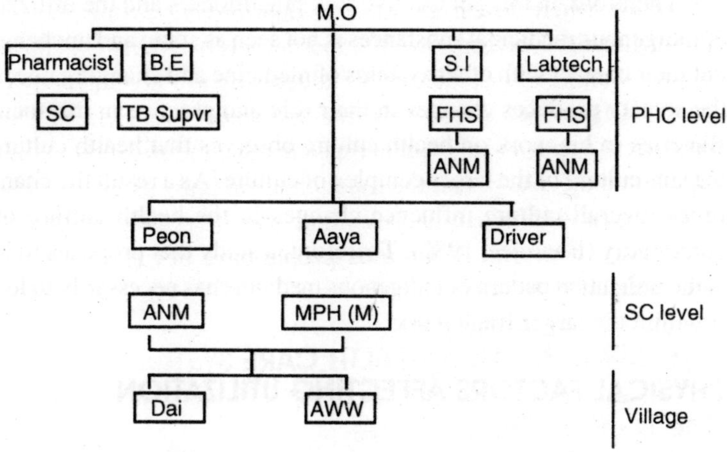

Fig. 6.1 : Institutional Structure of Primary Health Centre and Sub-Centre Level

UTILIZATION PATTERN OF INDIGENOUS MEDICINAL SUBSTANCES AND FACTORS AFFECTING IT

As our proposed study is concerned with tribal societies, special attention was given to the utilization of indigenous medicinal substances and the role of folk practitioners dealing with health problems in tribal societies. Since independence a number of changes have taken place, which had an impact on the lives of the tribals. These include the nature of development itself. Specific interventions through state agencies, which have had its effect on the livelihood, work; cultural practices, which include health seeking behaviour and this, have undergone change. Newer innovations and introduction of allopathic system of medicine have brought changes in the perception and practice not only in their various aspect of their life but also in their health seeking behaviour. They have started using the newer inventions since they have more choices when it comes to structures of provisioning in health. It is observed that the change in the larger socio-economic system is bound to produce changes in the subsystems. Our understanding is that the role of folk practitioners has to be conceptualized as part of the health care system, which is part of larger socio-economic system.

Therefore, in this perspective folk practitioners and the utilization of indigenous medicinal substances is not seen as static and unchanging but their contact with other systems of medicine and changing needs of the society produces changes in their role and practice in the society. Banerjee in his work on health culture observes that health culture is the sub-culture of the larger complex of culture. As a result the changes in the overall culture influence changes in the health culture of, a community (Banerjee, 1982). Therefore, a study that proposes to look at the utilization pattern of indigenous medicine has necessarily to locate it within the larger framework.

PHYSICAL FACTORS AFFECTING UTILIZATION

The distance between the two villages is around 30 km. Both of the villages are at a very far distance from the district hospital (around 130 km), which is located in the district headquarter. One road, i.e. the State highway connects Mualnuam and Thuangtam village to the district headquarters. If we starts from the district headquarters we reached Thuangtam village before Mualnuam village. However, Thuangtam village is much backward than Mualnuam village, which may be due to less population, infertile land, no basic amenities and above all irresponsible village chief. There is only one bus, which plies thrice in a week. When we examine the situation the utilization of indigenous medicine can be due to long physical distance between the villages and the district hospital, even though available but inaccessible for the villagers.

At the village level when we examine the resort pattern of respondents from Mualnuam village, the accessibility and availability of primary health centre, which is not functioning properly, and some medical store and the indigenous medicine demonstrates a clear influence for minor illnesses. There are variations in resort pattern. One finds that in Thuangtam village dependence on indigenous medicinal substances is much higher compared to Mualnuam village. This could probably be explained in terms of the availability and unavailability of health service infrastructure and that of accessibility and inaccessibility. It is extremely interesting to know that in Mualnuam village there is greater reliance in allopathic medicine. This kind of a trend reiterates the findings of Banerjee and Sahu who have made the point that while seeking relief from pain, people use services that are accessible and available to them.

Politico-economic factors affecting utilization

Our study shows that structure of provisions changed overtime. With the introduction of allopathic medicine the tribal are not resistance to their need and plurality of provisions reflected in plurality in utilization. For quick relief from illness, our study shows that majority of the people have a plural resort pattern. They used both the allopathic and indigenous medicine. The role of traditional practitioners and their practices have undergone changes with the introduction of allopathy. However, negligence by the government to provide medicine in the primary health center benefits the owner of small medical store while robbing the poor villagers of their hard earned money. The unstable political situation with corrupt politician, the health services system is totally not functioning in the rural areas. The attitude of the workers and doctors employed in rural areas is that of serving their superiors rather than the community. The workers too are more responsible to the targets of a particular programe than the welfare of the community.

The extent of focus on privatization of health services is also one of the reasons for decline use of government health facilities. It is understood that most of the curative services are provided by the private sector. But the idea of complete privatization of these services would, on the one hand, deviate from the concept of providing integrated health care services through the PHC approach. Secondly, privatization also leads to emphasise on cost recovery, thus the burden gradually shifting from the government to the individual consumer.

Socio-cultural factors affecting utilization

1. Beliefs

Religion, serves the central and crucial function in society of supporting what has been variously called social integration, social solidarity and social cohesion. Religion is an all-pervading supernatural phenomenon in man's life. For this reason perhaps it has been considered universal. Religion has exercised the most profound influence over man's thoughts and behaviour from times beyond human recollection.

Conversion to Christianity after the coming of the British missionaries has brought about changes in the family, marriage, social life of the Paites, their life styles, food habits, health seeking behaviour has also undergone significant changes. Before conversion to Christianity they believe in the existence of the spirits that move nature and guide human actions. They give different names to them and worship them in their own distinct way. The priests occupy a very important position and no ceremonies were performed without them. The priests also were considered as a great healer who heals people through his prayer and sacrifices of animals to Gods.

Among the tribal people, religion becomes all the more important for it is inter-woven in their entire social life and shapes most of their entire social behaviour. Thus, we can see the changes in the social behaviour encompassing the health culture or health seeking behaviour of the people in both the study villages. They stop believing in the religious sacrifices and healing practices of the priest or healers. But they continue to use indigenous medicinal substances for treating illnesses. In the beginning the priest/healers tried to oppose the change brought about by the new religion, but failed to do so as people stop approaching them and stop believing their healing powers.

Such kind of transformation of a society can be termed as 'social change'. " It is the significant alteration of social structures (that is, of patterns of social action and interaction) including consequences and manifestations of such structure embodied in norms (rules of conduct), values on cultural products and symbols. Social change is such a prevalent and often disturbing feature of contemporary life that both the specialist and the layman be tempted to suppose that it is peculiarly modern. Certainly the extent and rate of change in the modern world is greater than in most past periods. Change at some level and degree is a characteristic of man's life" (*International Encyclopaedia of Social Sciences*, Vol. XIV, 365). Thus, in a way we can see that the 'Paites' of both the study villages are undergoing a process of modernization where mental attitudes and institutional structures constitute the key elements in the process of modernization.

2. Occupation

The occupation of most of the respondents is cultivators. They *jhum* on the land given by the chief of the village. However with the coming in of State highway some of the villagers prefer doing their own private business like running a medical store, hotel, variety store, rice mill etc. With this increasing trend of exposure with the outside world, most of the villagers prefer using modern medicine and one can see that the indigenous medicinal substances are slowly dying out. They are considered inferior and ineffective as compared with the modern medicine.

3. Income of household

Income level is very much related to occupation. Even though there was no detail questioning on the amount of income received by a household, we can know it from the kind of assets, housing pattern and livestock they have. The utilization of private health services in the district headquarters increased with the increase in socio-economic standard/in income levels. The less privileged use the public health services like the district hospital in the district headquarters, or go to the local medical store. Those who does not have other source of income besides cultivation, goes to the PHC where they can get free medicine, otherwise they use indigenous medicinal substances, that too if they have the knowledge of using it.

4. Family size

The use of private as well as PHC/medical store showed a rising trend with the increase in family size and subsequently decrease in the use of PHC facility. This seems quite contradictory considering that poor families have larger households. An examination of the income structure of households revealed an increase in the family size (due to more numbers of earning members), explaining the utilization pattern of both allopathic and indigenous medicine. Thus, the family size and income level jointly seemed to affect the utilization pattern in the study area.

5. Education

A large number of respondents were illiterate or having lower levels of education upto the primary. Utilization of indigenous medicine has nothing much to do with education as the majority believe in it. However utilization of PHC facilities and medical store increased with levels of education. More illiterates sometimes just believe in the prescription of medical storeowners, without doctors or the pharmacist prescriptions. Education led to awareness and realization that self-medication can be dangerous for health. High percentage of illiterate women utilized both the PHC facility and the indigenous medicine. A predominant trend is also found among women that they avail to any treatment whether indigenous or modern, after 2-3 days of illness while relatively few resort to quick treatment to medical store /PHC (if open)/ indigenous medicinal substances. The low health awareness may be an attribute to the lower level of illiteracy and occupation as most of the women availing late medical help works in the field.

UTILIZER'S PERSPECTIVES OF CARE GIVERS

The villagers feel that the existence of indigenous practitioners should be there but not a healer who practices magico-spritual, as it is against their religious faith. Their faith in the healing power of indigenous medicinal substances is still very strong as they see positive result. However, they usually approach a modern health care facility in the first place and indigenous medicinal substances occupy an alternative position. The respondents also feel that the role of traditional healer/ folk practitioners has undergone change because there are no such full time practitioners available in both the villages.

Regarding the health personnel of the PHC, the respondents are of the view that they are unresponsive and irresponsible towards their duties. It has been observed that in the two villages fairly a significant number of people do not resort to care when they fall ill for both minor and major illnesses. Some of the reasons included are no doctor available nearby, no money, no time, improper treatment given by government doctors and the belief that allopathy cannot cure some of the diseases. These reasons points out that the caregivers lack responsiveness to specific illness or to the villagers' problem, rather than any resistance from the community to seek care. These kinds of observations were made by Banerjee and Anderson in the study of tuberculosis where they found that people do not go to the primary health centre as they did not get relief from the suffering caused by tuberculosis since they were dismissed with 'a bottle of cough mixture'. Here it is amply clear that the fault did not lie with the people who sought care but with an unresponsive health care system.

The service provider who are outside the public health care system, like the medical store man or private practitioners are perceived to be more responsible and effective by some of the utilizers. It is so, because none of the four employees and the Compounder, working in the PHC, are not residing in the village. They were either at the district headquarters or at the subdivisional headquarters where facilities are better. The study revealed that non-availability of basic modern amenities, remoteness of the village, lack of educational facilities for their children were the major reasons.

PROVIDER'S PERSPECTIVE

The perspective of the traditional practitioner

The in-depth interview with the only practitioner alive, shows that he stops practicing for the past one decade. His perception is that his role has undergone changes due to a number of factors, which are brought about by changes in the larger socio-economic milieu. These include resource depletion /over exploitation of the available resources that are plants and animals, the time taken in preparation of medicinal substances and besides this, the introduction of allopathic medicine together with Christianity. Beside this reason, he also feels that the community's response towards traditional practices especially belief in magical-spiritual healing, is no more relevant for them after conversion to Christianity. With these changes the people are more open to bring development in their villages. At the same time, they still utilized the indigenous medicinal substances available as an alternative to the allopathic medicine.

This mixed pattern of responses for both allopathy and indigenous medicine for both minor and major illnesses also contradicts much of the earlier anthropological works, which represent tribal as unaccepting of changes (in this case the introduction of allopathic medicine) since it does not share the same cultural world (Carstairs, 1955). It tends to represent them as people unwilling to change, therefore need to be "educated" about the importance of bio-medical world.

Perspective of the health personnel in the PHC

The list of problems faced by the PHC in village A is listed below :

- *Shortage of medicine/quality of medicines at the PHC.* Adequate supply of medicine was a problem in many PHCs and SCs. Discussion also indicated that shortage of medicines was partly due to the fact that medicines were distributed from the district panchayat to each PHC as per the population, rather than the performance of the OPD. At the same time the health personnel are least bothered of what happens to the supply, as no medicine means no work for them.
- *Infrastructure facilities at the PHC.* Observation of the PHC revealed that water supply/connection taken from the tanker, where spring water is stored, is not connected anymore. There is no power supply not only in the PHC but also in the whole village. There is no toilet facility. The PHC building was just constructed for showpiece. It lacked good maintenance.

Leaking roofs, lacked well-defined storage spaces and cleanliness. In fact the PHC building is left unused and whenever a doctor or medical official came for carrying out family planning programes, they used the house of the village Chief. The official at the PHC complained of limited powers in their hand, whereby they could not make modification to suit them. For any sort of replacement or facility required, a written application had to be submitted to the health department, and only at their order, could the work proceed. The long and cumbersome procedures delayed their implementation.

EMERGING ISSUES OF CONCERN FROM THE STUDY

To conclude from the discussions of the study, several constraints and potentials of the Primary Health Care system have been identified which affect the utilization and rendering of health services by the clients and providers respectively.

Constraints of the Primary Health Care System

The people of Mualnuam village do not face the problem of physical proximity towards the health centre. But lack of physical proximity of the health centre for Thuangtam village has been identified as a major constraint in utilization of the PHC, as they have to come to Mualnuam village, which is 30 km from their village. This is the nearest health centre, which Thuangtam village can avail. At the providers end, the same infrastructural bottleneck hinders rendering of services.

Dissatisfaction of the clients with the quality of medicines provided and the longer time taken to get cured, the unavailability of injections, the lesser timings for which the PHCs function, which is not suitable to their work timing in the field, all in contrast to the private outlets thwart the PHC's utilization. Lack of privacy during examination, the gender of the provider and the behaviour of the staff with the patients are other identified factors.

The programme driven supply of medicines, the meagre budget of the PHC for medicines and the excessive focus on achieving Family Planning and immunization targets further hamper the utilization of PHC for curative services. Women and children are considered important clientele for only these two services. But thére is insensitivity to their overall health problems. Thus the entire system is geared towards target fulfilment of preventive and promotive services, in the process, community involvement in identification of their health needs being neglected.

At the building level too, poor maintenance and unhygienic conditions, inefficiency in catering to emergency needs of deliveries, accidents and obstetric care become crucial in the rural population losing faith in the PHC system. The same issues at the providers' level such as lack of residential facility, poor maintenance in case of provision of residence, short of emergency skills at the PHC and SC level is an obstacle in providing good quality services. This further demotivates the doctors to work in rural areas.

The present system also fails to satisfy some other needs of its employees. Workers are not given salary in time due to the economic crisis in the State. Hence they became more irregular than before in delivering services to the people. They are more involved in target programmes and visit the village to implement the programmes, rather than working towards a more sustainable and holistic system. In spite of a good institutional structure, the approach remains bureaucratic, without satisfactory involvement of the community because of the failure of the PHC to reach the rural population for curative services.

Scope of indigenous medicine

The study reveals that the community prefers cheap and free medicines especially the poor families. However, the constraints and inefficiencies of the Public health delivery system is in a very sorry state with the needs of community looming large. In such a scenario the potentials and scope of the indigenous medicine and locally trained *Dais* become very important. The study also brings to light the preference of indigenous medicine or home made remedies and traditional healers by the respondents, especially the women, in the earlier stages of illness and also when they cannot pay for medicine. Their faith in this form of medicine can play a vital role in implementing the government's original plans of promoting Indian system of medicine in rural areas and at the same time recognizing the local tribal medicine.

The potential of the trained *dais, anganwadi* workers and traditional experts, if tapped can be instrumental in being a link between the community and health institution. Likewise, services of institutions from within the community, i.e., school teachers, religious institutions, private practitioners, women if tapped, can lead to successful implementation of the Primary Health Care goal of providing health services through community participation.

On the other hand the scope of indigenous medicine for improvement is on a very shaky ground. It is considered to be the last option when the modern scientific medicine has no answer. It is true that these indigenous medicines had functioned as viable 'primary health care' systems. This is adequately illustrated by the traditional systems that have served the needs of the people of India for centuries. Admitting the wholesomeness of some of the features of these traditional systems, the statement made by WHO that "they provide effective medical care to 80 percent of the total population" would appear to be much too generous, for it discounts the prevailing high incidence of preventable diseases and mortality, particularly infant and child mortality. These traditional systems have for quite some time past, been failing increasingly into disarray and their incapability to deal with changing health conditions cannot be ignored. Their present state is attributable partly to the inroads made by modern medicine into their domains and partly to their lack of adaptability to the changes that have been occurring in varied aspects of the social situation even in rural areas. Belief in their capacity to provide primary health care on their own is, accordingly, empty nostalgia, even when it is conceded that their rehabilitation and further development are feasible and desirable.

SUGGESTIONS

From the issues that emerged from the study it is clear that indigenous medicine is preferred as an alternative and not the first priority. The first priority being allopathic medicine or modern scientific medicine, this has explanation for every cause and effect. At the same time it does not mean that indigenous medicine is totally discarded. It is timeless and still close to people's heart. It is their indigenous knowledge linked to their culture, custom and tradition. However the impact of modern scientific medicine is quite tremendous that the belief in this system superseded the faith that people used to have in indigenous medicine. The outcome of this study shows that in the study villages the tribal people are hardly aware about government policy towards health care and also about the functions to be carried out by the primary health sub-centre. The indigenous systems that the government tries to promote are Ayurved and Homoeopathy, which is quite irrelevant for the tribal people given a choice between their own tribal medicine and Indian System of Medicine (ISM) they will go for their own tribal medicine. It means they have faith in only allopathic medicine when it comes to seeking treatment outside their indigenous medicine. In other words, what the government tries to promote as indigenous medicine in compliance with the declaration of WHO is not indigenous for many of the tribals living in India, if not for all the tribals but it is for tribes under this study. In the annual plan of Health Department of Manipur Government (2002-03), it was stated that 'the scheme for establishment of homoeopathic and ayurvedic clinics targeted during the Eighth and Ninth Plan could not be achieved due to non-creation of posts. Seven posts created during the Seventh Plan are still maintained under the plan.' It further states that 'but so far none of the clinics could be established due to financial constraints'. The scheme of ISM and Homoeopathy has been covered under Prime Minister Gram Yojana (PMGY) with effect from 2000-01. If this is the kind of promotion / attention being given to the Indian System of Medicine recognized officially it is hard to imagine when will the localized medicine get recognition and promotion from the government.

The reality in the field situation is quite thought provoking. The policies and plans of the government seem to be a policy and plans to read and listen but not to implement. If by chance implementation becomes successful it is well and good and if not it means blame on technical default or financial constraints or lack of personnel. Thus the study wants to suggest that modern medicine is not here only for the elite. But until government decides that all their people are entitled to the best care that modern medicine has to offer we will still be debating whether indigenous medicine is better than modern or scientific medicine. It is when we are desperate that we will rely on indigenous medicine, assume the dependent role, and trust magic.

One can understand that patients become desperate and resorting to this kind of behaviour, but why international organizations like the WHO also play this role. Partly because they are expected to play it when the situation demands it and partly because the planners faith in science is still on shaky grounds. It has been only 150 years since he came out of his shamanistic roots. When the pressure is on, there is a tendency to abandon belief in the scientific method and resort to pseudo-science. In brief it shows that WHO is very much desperate to attain the goal of 'health for all' that it sought all possible means and options. However it seems that little progress has been made in actually utilizing indigenous health practitioners or in improving the indigenous medicine itself. It appears in fact that in entire developing world there are only one or two countries in which traditional healers and their medicine have actually been incorporated in the National health care system. Thus the big question is if the policy is there, why then is it so little implemented and how should outcomes be evaluated when it is? Some indigenous therapies may be helpful, some may have no effect, and some may be harmful. Even the ones that are efficacious may not be as efficacious as allopathic medicine might offer. And some may be better than Western medicine. But we will never know the answer unless we start to do outcome studies.

CONCLUSION

The worldwide interest in the use of natural products and plant-based remedies has led to different situations developing in different countries. In countries with a strong foundation of indigenous medicine such as India and China, nationally recognized parallel traditional systems have run for long periods, along with Western medicine with varying degrees of acceptance, integration and assimilation. In other countries like those in Africa, there is now a move to give legitimacy to the traditional healer whose medical practice has been the mainstay of the local people, even after Western medicine made its appearance and took firm roots. In Europe and USA, a new and growing consumer interest in the use of natural medicine and herbal products have opened burgeoning markets for health promotion products aimed at the improvement of physical well-being. This is a comparatively new constituency of herbal medicine users for prevention of diseases rather than cures for illnesses. Their emphasis has been on the use of single herbs and therapies promoted by consumer interest and demand and not yet fully understood or recognized by governments, including drug authorities. Meanwhile, a strong consumer demand for herbal products, plant based remedies and a growing interest in the indigenous medicine, for example in Ayurveda, Acupuncture, Chinese medicine etc. that are millennia old, is taking place.

Countries today, the worldover, are flooded with thousands of plant-based remedies, which have entered the markets as food supplements. Such products, which are primarily plant based and may or may not contain synthetic ingredients, are being freely manufactured and exported. Many of the remedies have their roots in the use of plants for their medicinal value. In this process medicinal plants growing in the wild are extracted illegally that it is on the verge of extinction. At the same time the tribals in the forest are forced to go deeper into the wild forest to extract wild medicinal plants but are given a little share of the entire value of the plants they extracted. With the growth of consumer demand on the one hand and the current socio-political ideologies on the other, governments have been trying to grapple with the task of approaching indigenous medicine, its products and practitioners in a way that can be simple and meaningful enough to make a significant improvement to people's daily live while ensuring safety. In this pursuit, the government has naturally to confer legitimacy only on such systems, practices, therapies and drugs, which have been investigated and found to be efficacious and assured. This exercise, however, calls for the integration of several facets, which go into the making, and practice of indigenous medicine, which requires an understanding of the sector, its strengths and weaknesses and what will work.

Indigenous medicine in every country wherever it has a strong base, has emerged out of an individual physician's approach to the problems of an individual patient spreading to the family, and later the community. Rooted in indigenous medicine is the belief that every person belongs to a broad stereotype and problems can be treated by understanding the individual's personal traits and specific factors, which have brought about disequilibrium. Whereas allopathic medicine has a reductionistic approach and looks upon the removal of the symptoms of disease as the main objective but indigenous medicine does not see only a single remedy or a single approach as being suitable for all people. Symptoms are seen only as an indication of a deeper malaise, which is necessarily not considered to be caused by physiological factors alone.

POLICY RECOMMENDATION

From the field study we find that in terms of priorities, the epidemiological situation compels governments to confront basic public health problems, leaving little time, space or funds for including indigenous medicinal approaches, which are necessarily individualistic, slow and difficult to monitor and evaluate. On yet another plane lies the clinical approach, extended through allopathic dispensaries and hospitals designed to treat individual and specialized problems with modern diagnostics and drugs. In other words, by legitimizing indigenous healing practices (which have a wide spectrum from beneficial to outright dangerous or even fatal), the World Health Organization is pandering to nationalistic pride but will fail to deal with real health problems it might otherwise have done. In effect it may be settling for secondary rate medicine. Modern medicine is not here only for the elite. But until government decides that all their people are entitled to the best care that modern medicine has to offer we will still be debating whether indigenous medicine is better than modern or scientific medicine. It is when we are desperate that we will rely on indigenous medicine, assume the dependent role, and trust magic.

With such a wide difference in concepts and approaches between indigenous and modern medicine, the research study could not come up with proper suggestions but has come up with more queries in regard to legitimizing and promoting indigenous medicine that calls for attention of policy makers. Is it at all possible to bring about any kind of integration, which would be of significant benefit to the people? Are comparisons between the losses of productivity on the one hand (which invariably calls for strong medication) and the elimination of side effects on the other (albeit with gentler but slower traditional drugs) at all possible? Can one weigh the short-term benefits of getting back to work over the long-term benefits of avoiding dependence on strong drugs and resistance patterns? Is there at all a case for identifying which part of the indigenous systems can be integrated into a health system? Where does indigenous medicine fall between the public health approach on the one hand and the specialist-driven hospital-based approach on the other? Where will the inclusion of indigenous medicine work to the greatest advantage, and can there be a policy on its integration into the health system?

To be serious in adapting indigenous systems of medicine it is necessary to first get into its essence. This is the challenge of getting into its core even before thinking of "using" it and manipulating it. The situation of our country offers special challenge. This old civilization, with rich and diversified cultural heritage, with different religion, tradition and ethnic groups, needs to be thoroughly screened and more research needs to be done before any health care planning is envisaged. Also making any policy in favour of them calls for a very close scrutiny with all their positive and negative components on the one hand and a careful incorporation of them in the health care delivery on the other. If not, our own selfishness that is developing for one's sake will only drown us. There is a danger of getting into superficialities of things that tend to blind us. We have to get into the core and experience its totality and not just a part of it. Then we will never left without direction.

These are some of the issues which policy makers administering the health sector have to grapple with, and at the back of every decision making process lies the question of whether the alternative offered by indigenous medicine will lead to a significant improvement over the current situation, sufficient to call for a change of policy. Would government like to introduce strategies which may suit the individual but which may lead to delay in the diagnosis of a really serious illness? How can the expertise of the practitioner and the quality and safety of the drugs be assured? Would government be in a position to introduce regulations and enforcement mechanisms that protect the patient against malpractice and spurious drugs, without curbing the individuality of the practitioner? Equally, should the consumer be denied access to simpler, gentler forms of treatment only because there is no one to inform him about such alternatives? If at all indigenous medicine is to be used as a strategy to bolster the normal health care approach, where will its inclusion make the greatest impact and how can such assimilation take place?

At this time when there is global consciousness towards indigenous knowledge, it is crucial to stop for a while and contemplate again on the basic question that one has to answer before starting again. Why are we doing this? For whom? For what? And from the vision will be carved out answers to those questions.

REFERENCE

Carstairs, G.M. 1955. "Medicine and Faith in Rural Rajasthan" In Paul, P.D. (ed) *Health, Culture and Community*, New York, Russell Sage Foundation.

International Encyclopaedia of Social Sciences. 1978. Vol. XIV, pp.365.

APPENDIX - I

Hill Tribes of Manipur

Manipur is divided into Hills and Plain Districts. The tribals who are recognized as the Scheduled Tribes of India mainly occupy the Hill Districts. Out of so many tribes listed below Paite tribe is selected for the study. The Hill Tribes of Manipur can be divided as listed below :

NAGA TRIBE

(a) Tangkhuls
(b) Mao
(c) Anal
(d) Angami
(e) Kabui
(f) Kacha Naga
(g) Maram
(h) Maring
(i) Monsang
(j) Moyon
(k) Lamgang
(l) Koirao
(m) Koireng
(n) Sema

KUKI-CHIN TRIBE

(a) Aimol
(b) Chiru
(c) Chothe
(d) Gangte
(e) Hmar
(f) Kom
g) Paite*
(h) Purum
(i) Ralte
(j) Simte
(k) Thadou
(l) Vaiphei
(m) Zou
(n) Any Mizo (Lushai tribe)
(o) Sahte

---

* The study Tribe

APPENDIX - II

Some of the Medicinal Plants Found in Churachandpur District

S.No.	Local Name	Scientific Name	Familes	English Name
1.	Aieng	*Curcuma domestica*	Zingiberaceae	Turmeric
2.	Ailaidum	*Curcuma caesia roxb.*	Zingiberaceae	Black Zeodoary
3.	Aital	*Amomum subulatum roxb.*	Zingiberaceae	Nepal cardamom
4.	Aksipak	*Ervatmia coronaria stapf.*	Apocynaceae	East Indian rose bay
5.	Anbong	*Rumex vasicarius linn.*	Polygonaceae	Bladder dock
6.	Ankam tobawk	*Brassica rapa linn*	Brassicaceae	Common turnip
7.	Ankambulbalzen	*Raphanus salivus linn*	Brassicaceae	Raddish
8.	Ankam bulbal eng Sativa Dc.	*Daucus carota linn var*	Apiaceae	Carrot
9.	Ankam bul khumte	*Beta vulgaris linn*	Chenopodiaceae	Beet root
10.	Ankam ngou/ kamkuak	*Lactuca sativa linn*	Asteraceae	Garden lettuce
11.	Anphui	*Clerodendrum indicum (linn) kuntze*	Verbenaceae	
12.	Anthul	*Hisbiscus sabdarriffa linn*	Malvaceae	Red sorret
13.	Bilthei	*Aegle marmelos correa ex robx.*	Rutaceae	Baet tree
14.	Aipak	*Asparagus racemosus wild*	Liliaceae	Asparagus
15.	Akektehsing	*Holarrhena antidy sentirica*	Apocynaceae	
16.	Bawngek loulian	*Amaranthus viridus*	Amarathaceae	Wild amaranth
17.	Dailuah	*Lens culinaris medic*	Papilionaceae	Lentil
18.	Dawnpawl	*Citrullus vulgaris schrad*	Cucurbitaceae	Watermelon
19.	Gam lengthei	*Pandanus tectorius*	Amarllidaceae	
20.	Gam sahawk	*Citrus grandis*	Rutaceae	
21.	Ganja	*Cannabis sativa linn*	Cannabinaceae	Truehemp Marijuana
22.	Gokha	*Teinostachyum weightei*	Poaceae	Thorny bamboo
23.	Hakaisan	*Dioscorea alata linn*	Dioscoreaceae	Asiatic yam
24.	Helsesing	*Mesua ferrea linn*	Clusiaceae	Iron wood
25.	Iskut	*Cucurbita pepo linn*	Cucurbitaceae	Vegetable marrow
26.	Kani	*Papaver somniferum linn*	Papaveraceae	Opium poppy
27.	Kawlkai	*Ipomoea batatas (linn) lamk*	Convoluilaceae	Sweet potato
28.	Kawltu	*Saccharum offinarum linn*	Poaceae	Sugarcane
29.	Kawlsing	*Psidium guajava linn*	Myrtaceae	Common guava
30.	Khuanglang	*Ficus religiosa linn*	Moraceae	Peepal

S.No.	Local Name	Scientific Name	Familes	English Name
31.	Kofi	*Coffea arabica linn*	Rubiaceae	Arabian coffee
32.	Khongma	*Rhus semialata murr syn. R. chinensis mills*	Anarcardiaceae	
33.	Lamkhuang	*Arlocarpus integrifolia linn*	Moraceae	Jack tree
34.	Leenmui	*Syzygium cuminii(linn) skeela*	Myrtaceae	Black plum
35.	Leengpigah	*Vitis vinefara linn*	Vitaceae	Grape vine
36.	Loupa hoih(nahngat)	*Cynodon dactylon pers*	Poaceae	Dhub grass
37.	Lunmui	*Ocimum canumsims*	Lamiaceae	Hoary basil
38.	Makha	*Juglans regia linn*	Juglandaceae	
39.	Mangpuangsing gum	*Eucalyptus globules labile*	Myrtaceae	Tasmanianblue eucalypt
40.	Meiteilou	*Ageratum conyzoides linn*	Asteraceae	Goat weed
41.	Mualvaiseek	*Citrus jambhori*	Rutaceae	
42.	Muchih/Musi	*Ricinus communis linn*	Euphorbiaceae	Castor seed
43.	Pasi	*Schizophyllum communa Fr*	Agarocaceae	
44.	Pateh	*Agaricus*	Agaricaceae	
45.	Phulunngou	*Allium sativum*	Liliaceae	Garlic
46.	Pudina	*Mentha arvensis linn*	Poaceae	Field mint
47.	Saidaikung, sailengthei	*Agave Americana linn*	Agavaceae	Century plant, American aloe
48.	Saiseek	*Citrus maxima*	Rutaceae	Pummelo
49.	Samphokneu	*Solanum nigrum linn*	Solanaceae	Black night shade
50.	Samphokpi	*Solanum torum*	Solanaceae	
51.	Seekkhum	*citrus reticulata blanco*	Rutaceae	Bigarade orange lime
52.	Siing	*Zingiber officinale rose*	Zingiberaceae	Ginger plant
53.	Singguithak	*Cinamomum Zeylanicum*	Lauraceae	
54.	Singmalta	*Piper longum linn*	Piperaceae	Indian long pepper
55.	Singtangmai	*Carica papaya linn*	Moraceae	Papaya
56.	Suaklu	*Emblica offinalis gaertn*	Euphorbiaceae	Emblicmyrobalan/ goose berry
57.	Tangkha	*Momordica charantica linn*	Cucurbitaceae	Bitter gourd
58.	Tangkuangteh	*Centella asiatica linn syn.*	Apiaceae	Asiatic pennywort
59.	Tangsaamteh	*Eupartorium birmani cum DC*	Asteraceae	
60.	Theiantang	*Punica granatum linn*	Punicaceae	Pomegranate
61.	Theimul/meitei thei	*Prunus persica(linn) batsch*	Rosaceae	Peach
62.	Theipi	*Ficus cunia buch ham*	Moraceae	Fig tree
63.	Tawnniang	*Cyperus rotundus linn*	Cyperaceae	Nut grass
64.	Vandawtsing	*Terminalia bellerica (gaertn)*	Combretaceae	
65.	Zanah /Dum	*Nicotiana tobacum linn*	Solanaceae	Tobacco

APPENDIX - III

Some of the Medicinal Substances Existing in both the Villages

In traditional medical practice, generally the plants are often used in a compound form to which other herbs, metals, minerals and animal products are added. These plants are generally available from forests, fields, roadsides, grocer shops and even from the kitchen. These medicinal substances are processed in several ways before administration to a patient. Those, which are done by the villagers at home described below:

(1) Curcuma Domestica/Longa

English name: Turmeric
Local name: Aieng
Parts used: Rhizome
Habitat: Cultivated throughout tropical regions
Description: A tall herb, about 60-cm high with large oblong leaves. Flowers appear in rainy season.
Therapeutic uses: Externally it is used in the treatment of scabies, itches, boils, abscess, eczema and eye diseases. Internally it is used for cough, cold and fever, especially for mothers after delivery.
Mode of administration: For external use, the paste administration is rubbed like an ointment.

(2) Curcuma Caesia Roxb

English name: Black Zedoary
Local name: Ailaidum
Description: (similar with turmeric but roots are brownish)
Parts used: Rhizome (roots)
Therapeutic uses: Stomachache or acidity problem
Mode of administration: The powder is mixed with water or honey and consumed.

(3) Aegle Markelos

English name: Bael tree
Local name: Bilthei
Parts used: Fruit, leaf and bark of stem as well as root
Habitat: It grows in tropical forests as well as in plains
Description: It is a tree about 7-9 metres high. The leaf has three leaflets and when crushed it produces a typical aroma. Fruits are oval, oblong or roundish. Colour of the fruit is light green but when ripe, it is light yellow or brown.
Therapeutic uses: Bael fruits are used in the treatment of diarrhoea, dysentery, and loss of appetite. It is safely given to children. Also used in treatment of constipation.
Mode of administration: Both unripe and ripe fruits are used. Unripe fruits are cut into thin slices, dried in the sun and made powder. This is taken by mixing with water.

(4) Holarrhena Antidysenterica

Local name: Ak ek tehsing
Parts used: Bark
Habitat: Grows wild in tropical forests
Description: It is a tree of 3-4.5 m high. Leaves are elongated. Flowers are white or pink. Fruits are slender, elongated and about

25 cm long. Fruits appear in bunches.

Therapeutic uses: It is used in treatment of diarrhoea and dysentery.

Mode of administration: Bark is used in the form of powder or decoction. It is very bitter in taste. To overcome this they add some sugar or honey to the powder or decoction.

(5) Ficus Reliogiosa

English name: Peepal tree, sacred tree

Local name: Khuanglang

Parts used: Stem bark

Habitat: Grows wild in tropical and sub-tropical areas.

Description: It is a big tree. Leaf blade is round and tapering, and the apex, which looks like a tapering tail, is one-third of the blade.

Therapeutic uses: Used for bleeding gums, pus in the gums and swelling of the mouth and tongue. Slender stems are used as toothbrush.

Mode of administration: Powder of the stem bark is used as tooth powder. The decoction of the stem bark is used for mouthwash.

(6) Cynodon Dactylon

English name: Dhub grass

Local name: Loupa hoih (nahngat)

Parts used: Entire plant

Habitat: It is found in nature, hedges and fields.

Description: It is a creeping grass, which spreads on the ground. Roots came out from each stem-joint. Leaves are long and slender in shape and green or white in colour.

Therapeutic uses: It stops bleeding. It is used in bleeding piles and leucorrhoea (white and foul smelling discharge from the female genital tract).

Mode of administration: Its paste or juice is used externally to stop bleeding from external wounds. To stop bleeding from the nose, its juice is dropped into the nose. Internally, it is used in the form of paste or juice. Since it is commonly available round the year, it is not difficult to collect fresh herb for use everyday.

(7) Emblica Officinalis

English name: Gooseberry

Local name: Suaklu

Parts used: Fruit

Habitat: It grows wild in forests and cultivated in plains of tropical and sub-tropical areas.

Description: It is a tree 6-7.5 m high. Fruits are round, fleshy and greenish yellow in colour. Dried fruits are brownish black in colour.

Therapeutic uses: It is often used as tonic, specially for children, also used in treatment of acidity in the stomach, vomiting (specially during pregnancy) and burning urination.

Mode of administration: Generally used in the form of paste, juice powder or decoction.

(8) Centella Asiatica

English name: Asiatic pennywort

Local name: Tang kuang the

Parts used: Generally found their water reservoirs and streams of water in the tropics and temperate climate.

Description: It is a creeper. It spreads over on the ground. From each node of the stem, leaves, roots and flowers emerge. Leaves are green in colour and round in shape with a depression at the centre.

Therapeutic uses: Used as a tonic and in the treatment of convulsive disorders, also used in the treatment of diabetes.

Mode of administration: It is used in the form of paste, juice or powder. The decoction is most popular among the villagers. It is also consume as vegetable or salad.

(9) Eupartorium Birmanicum DC

Local name: Tangsaam

Parts used: Leaves

Habitat: It is found in nature, hedges, roadsides, and fields.

Description: It is a tree with slender branches of adequate height (not very tall).

Therapeutic uses: It is used for the treatment of wounds and cuts.

Mode of administration: It is used in the form of paste. The paste is applied on the cuts or wounds.

(10) Ricinus Communis

English name: Castor seed

Local name: Muchih/Musi

Parts used: Root, seed, leaf and oil.

Habitat: It grows in tropical, sub-tropical and temperate regions.

Description: It is a bush or occasionally a soft-wooden small tree up to 6 m high. Leaves are green or reddish. Flowers appear in spikes of 30-60 cm.

Therapeutic uses: For treatment of joint pains, the oil from the seed is used externally and internally.

Mode of administration: The castor oil is given in small doses internally. Leaves are made warm by exposure to fire, and then applied over the affected joints.

(11) Messua Ferrea

English name: Iron wood tree

Local name: Helsesing

Parts used: Flowers

Description: It is a tree of about 6 m high. Stem bark is reddish. Flowers appear in bunches.

Therapeutic uses: It is used externally for scabies and eczema. It is used internally for excessive menstrual bleeding and leucorrhoea (white discharge from the female genital tract).

Mode of administration: It is used internally in powder form. For external use, a fine paste is prepared from its flowers and buds by adding water. The paste is applied on the affected part.

Mixture of Plants and Animals

(1) *Ingredients:* A dead Scorpion (or in the family of scorpion that is poisonous), is soak in 'Zu' (wine made from local rice) for as long as possible (no time limit).
Therapeutic uses: The 'Zu' is consumed but not the scorpion. It is used for treatment of cancer.

(2) *Ingredients:* Crab and banana's flower
Methods of preparation: Crab and the flowers of banana that is cut into small pieces are cooked properly. The decoction or the soup is consumed.
Therapeutic uses: It is used for the treatment of jaundice or problem related to liver.

(3) *Ingredients:* Prone (red in colour after drying)
Therapeutic uses: It is use for treating mumps
Preparation: The raw prone is grind, wrap in a cloth and pat on the affected area for a long time.

(4) *Ingredients:* Snake's liver
Therapeutic use: Dysentery and diarrhoea
Preparation: Small part of the preserved liver is grind, mixed with water, honey, or sugar, and then consumed.
Local name: Gulpi sinkha.

(5) *Ingredients:* Tuikep (local name)
English name: not exactly known but can be included in snail's family
Therapeutic uses: It is used in serious cases of burns, proved to be very effective, no scar remain after regular application
Preparation: The cover or the skin of 'tuikep' is exposed to fire, then grind it into powder and apply the powder on the affected areas.

APPENDIX - IV

Interview Schedule for the People Community

Name of the Village

Name of the Tribe/Caste

1. Name of the respondents :
2. Religion :
   (a) Hindu
   (b) Muslim
   (c) Christian
   (d) Others (specify)
3. Knowledge of Languages:
4. Education
   (a) Illiterate
   (b) Below 5th class
   (c) Below 10th class
   (d) Above 10th class (specify)
   (e) Adult education
5. Occupation :
   (a) Agriculture
   (b) Private sector
   (c) Public sector

(d) Self-employed

6. Type of housing and assets:
   (a) Kucha/ pucca/semi-pucca
   (b) Latrine yes/ no (if yes, type)
   (c) Electricity
   (d) Radio
   (e) Television
   (f) Vehicle/ Bicycle/Two wheeler/Four wheeler
   (g) Others (specify)
7. Live stock:
   (a) Cow
   (b) Buffalo
   (c) Pig
   (d) Horse
   (e) Goats
   (f) Sheep
   (g) Others (specify)
8. Type of family: Joint / Nuclear
9. Family details:

S.No.	Family Members	Name	Sex	Age	Education	Self-Reported Illness	Resort

10. What according to you are the general health problems in your area/locality?
11. What do you think what are the causes of illness?
    (a) Minor (cough, cold, loose motion, fever etc.)
    (b) Major (hospitalized)

12. Have you or any of your family members experienced any health problem in last one year?
13. Where did you go for treatment?
14. How did you treat your illness/ailments (minor as well as major)?
15. What are the major health problems you had in last one year, which needed hospitalization?
16. Where did you go?
17. Which service do you resort to most often in case of :
    (a) Minor illness
        ☞ Traditional medicine
        ☞ Private practitioners
        ☞ Primary health centre / district hospital
    (b) Major illness
        ☞ Traditional medicine
        ☞ Private practitioners
        ☞ Primary health centre/ district hospital
18. Which services do you consider better? Why?
19. Who are the significant traditional healers available in your village?
20. Under what condition do you go to a traditional healer?
21. Under what condition do you use your own knowledge of indigenous medicine?
22. How responsible are the traditional healers in treating illness?
23. Do you think that the utilization of traditional healers and indigenous substances play an important role in maintaining the health of the community?
24. Has the role of traditional healers changed during the last two decades? (Yes/no, then how?)
25. What types of medicinal plants are found in your village?
26. Are the medicinal plants or substances easily available and accessible?

27. According to you which type of medicine is the most costly? Please rank the following in order of cost.
    (a) Allopathy
    (b) Homoeopathy
    (c) Ayurvedic
    (d) Indigenous medicinal substances

APPENDIX - V

Interview Schedule for the Traditional Practitioners/Healers

Name of the Village

Name of the Tribe/Caste

1. Name of the respondents:
2. Religion:
   (a) Hindu
   (b) Muslim
   (c) Christian
   (d) Others (specify)
3. Knowledge of Languages:
4. Education
   (a) Illiterate
   (b) Below 5th class
   (c) Below 10th class
   (d) Above 10th class (specify)
   (e) Adult education
5. Occupation:
   (a) Agriculture
   (b) Private sector

(c) Public sector
(d) Self-employed

6. Type of housing and assets:
(a) Kucha/ pucca/semi-pucca
(b) Latrine yes/ no (if yes, type)
(c) Electricity
(d) Radio
(e) Television
(f) Vehicle/ Bicycle/ Two wheeler/ Four wheeler
(g) Others (specify)

7. Live stock:
(a) Cow
(b) Buffalo
(c) Pig
(d) Horse
(e) Goats
(f) Sheep
(g) Others (specify)

8. Type of family: Joint / Nuclear

9. Family details:

S.No.	Family Members	Name	Sex	Age	Education	Self-Reported Illness	Resort

10. What according to you are the general health problems in your area/locality?

11. What do you think what are the causes of illness?
(a) Minor (cough, cold, loose motion, fever etc.)
(b) Major (hospitalized)

12. Were there any practitioner in your family? If yes, - who?

13. How was the practice then, different from now? Please explain.
14. What kind of illnesses do you heal? (Your specialization)
15. Why did you choose this profession?
16. Are you a part-time or full-time practitioner?
17. Is there any preference among men and women while choosing this profession?
18. What is your opinion about allopathic system or other system of medicine?
19. For what kind of ailments do people come to you for treatment?
20. What kind of medicinal substances do you mainly used for treatment?
21. Are these medicinal substances easily accessible and available in your area?
22. Do you think that the medicinal substances needs more exploration or are they on the verge of extinction?
23. Do you approved in cultivation of medicinal plants? Why?
24. Are you given an important role and status in the community to perform your duties?
25. What is your role in activities other than treating illness?
26. How do you perceive your social status in society given your role as traditional healer?
    (a) Very high
    (b) High
    (c) Mediocre
    (d) Low
    (e) Very low
27. What is/are your suggestion (s) for improving your skill?
28. Do you see any threat from other health care system? Reason.

APPENDIX - VI

Interview Schedule for the Health Personnel at Sub-centre

(1) Name of the respondent:

(2) Designation:

(3) Place:

(4) How long have you been working here?

(5) Are people from-------- village utilize the services of the PHSC*?

  (a) Approximately what percentage of the population uses your services?

  (b) Who from these villages use the PHSC more? Male/ female/children

  (c) How do they react to your prescribed treatment?

(6) For what kind of minor/major illnesses do people come to the PHSC?

(7) What is the attitude of the people towards PHSC?

(8) Is there any change in their attitude over the years?

(9) What do you feel about the other system of medicine?

(10) How significant is the role-played by the traditional practitioners / healers?

(11) What kind of ailment do they normally treat?

---

* PHSC — primary health sub-centre

(12) What kind of problem do you face while rendering your duties?

(13) How is the community's response towards National Health Programmes?

Bibliography

Agrawal, Pradeep, Saibaba, P. "TRIPS and India's Pharmaceuticals Industry", *Economic and Political Weekly*, September 29, pp. 3787-3790.

Anaya, S. James. 1996. *Indigenous Peoples in International Law*. New York, USA: Oxford University Press.

Banerjee, D. 1979. "Place of the Indigenous and the Western systems of Medicine in the health services of India", *International Journal of Health Services*, Volume 9, Number 3, pp. 511-519.

Banerjee, Madhulika. 2000. "Whither Indigenous Medicine", *Seminar*, 480, May, pp.44-48.

Banerji, D. 1985. *Poverty, Class and Health Culture in India*, Volume 1, New Delhi: Prachi Prakashan.

Banerji, D. 1995. *Health and Family Planning Services in India*, New Delhi: Lok Paksh Publications.

Banerji, D. and Anderson, S. 1982. "A Sociological study of the awareness of symptoms suggestive of pulmonary tuberculosis", *Bulletin of WHO*, 23.

Bannerman, Robert H. 1983. *Traditional Medicine and Health Care Coverage*, Geneva: World Health Organization.

Bibeau, Gilles. 1985. "From China to Africa: The Same Impossible Synthesis between Traditional and Western Medicines", *Social Science and Medicine*, Vol. 21, No. 8, pp. 937-943.

Blackburn, T.C. and Anderson, K. (Ed). 1993. *Before the wilderness: Environmental management by native Californians*. Menlo Park, California, USA: Ballena Press.

Bodekar, Gerard. 1994. "Traditional Health Care and Public Policy: Recent Trend", *Workshop paper, IDRC*, pp.96-108.

Bonabeau, E. and Theraulaz, G. 1994, *Intelligence Collective*, Paris: Hermes.

Bose, Ashish and Desai. 1983. *Studies in Social Dynamics of Primary Health Care*, Delhi, India: Hindustan Publishing Corporation.

Bose, Ashish, Tiplut Nongbri, Nishlesh Kumar. 1990. *Tribal Demography and Development in North-East India*, New Delhi: B.R. Publishing Corporation.

Brehony, Eamonn. 2000. "Whose practice counts? Experiences in using indigenous health practices from Ethiopia and Uganda", *Development in Practice*, Vol.10, No. 5, November, pp. 650-661.

Carstairs, G.M. 1955. "Medicine and Faith in rural Rajasthan" In Paul P.D. (ed) *Health, Culture and Community*, New York: Russell Sage Foundation.

CERPA. 2001-02. "Demand Study for Selected Medicinal Plants", *CERPA (Centre for Research, Planning and Action)*, New Delhi.

Commission on Intellectual Property Rights. 2002. "Integrating Intellectual Property Rights and Development Policy", *Report of the Commission on Intellectual Property Rights.*

Correa, Carlos M. 2000. *Intellectual Property Rights, the WTO and Developing Countries: The TRIPS Agreement and Policy Options*, London : Zed Books Ltd., pp. 5-6.

Correa, Carlos M. 2000. "In situ conservation and Intellectual Property Rights", in Brush, S. (Ed) *Genes in the field. On-farm conservation of crop diversity*, IPGRI/IDRC: Lewis Publishers.

Cox, P.A. 1997. "Indigenous peoples and conservation", In F. Grifo and J. Rosenthal (Ed), *Biodiversity and Human Health*, Covelo, California, USA: Island Press, pp. 207-220.

Chandra, Shailaja. 2000 (a). "Can Public Health and Traditional Medicine meet or mix?" *Health for the Millions*, September-October, pp. 16-19.

Chandra, Shailaja. 2000 (b). "Traditional Systems of Medicine and Public Health", *Health for the Millions*, May-June, pp. 8-12.

Charles, Molly. 2001. "Drug trade in Himachal Pradesh— Role of Socio-economic Changes", *Economic and Political Weekly*, June 30, pp. 2433-2439.

Chaudhuri, Buddhadeb. 2002. "Traditional Knowledge and Wisdom— Relevance in the Present Day World", *Geographical Review of India*, June, Vol. 64, No.2, pp. 157-164.

Chinkhanshyam, T. and S. Thanmang. 2000. "Zougam Flora", Directorate for Development of Tribal and Backward Classes, Government of Manipur.

Datta, S.K. 2001. "Marketing of Wild Medicinal Plants Tribal Economy in India", *Economic and Political Weekly*, September 22, pp.3598-3602.

Daes, E.I.A. 1999. "Human rights of Indigenous peoples: Indigenous people and their relationship to land", Second progress report on the working paper. E/CN.4/Sub.2/1999/ 18. Sub-Commission on Prevention of Discrimination and Protection of Minorities, United Nations Commission on Human Rights, Geneva, Switzerland.

Dasmann, R.F. 1988. "Towards a Biosphere Consciousness", In D. Worster (Ed) *The Ends of the Earth: Perspective on Modern Environmental History*, Cambridge University Press, pp. 177-188.

Durkheim, Emile. 1961. *Moral Education*, New York: The Free Press.

Dutfield, G. 2000a. "Intellectual property rights, trade and biodiversity", International Union for the Conservation of Nature (IUCN), London.

Editorial. 1997. "Cultivation of medicinal plants—Conservation charade", *Amruth*, August, pp.11-14 (Published by Foundation for Revitalization of Local Health Traditions).

Editorial. 2001. "Drug Patents and Public Health", *Economic and Political Weekly*, March 10, pp.795-796.

Editorial. 2001, "Trading in contraband", *Down to Earth*, January, pp. 38-41.

Emmel, N.D. 1998. "Health-for-All for 21st Century Demise of Primary Health Care", *Economic and Political Weekly*, March 14, pp. 577-580.

Gadgil, M. 1995. "Prudence and profligacy: A human ecological perspective", In T.M. Swanson (Ed.), *The Economics and Ecology of Biodiversity Decline*, Cambridge University Press, pp. 99-110.

Gadgil, M. and Guha, R. 1992. *This Fissured Land.* Delhi: Oxford University Press.

Ghosh, Arun. 1996. "Health Care and Globalisation Case for a Selective Approach", *Economic and Political Weekly*, February 24, pp.441-442.

Glasser, Morton. 1988. "Accountability of Anthropologists, Indigenous Healers and their Governments: A plea for reasonable medicine", *Social Science and Medicine*, Vol. 27, No. 12, pp. 1461-1464.

Gopalakrishnan, R. and Singh, R.K. Rajan. 2001. *Constraints in Development of Manipur*, New Delhi: Regency Publications.

GOM 2001. Tenth Five Year Plan. 2002-2007, Directorate of Health Service, Department of Health and Family Planning, Govt. of Manipur.

Government of Manipur, *Annual Health Plan* (2002-2003); pp. 32-33.

Guite, Chinkholian.1999. *Politico-economic development of the tribals of Manipur*, New Delhi: Anmol Publication Pvt. Ltd.

Gunatilleke, Godfrey, P.D.A. Perera, Joel Fernandes, Eardley Fernando. 1988. *Seasonality and Health* (a study of the socio-economic environment of ill health in five locations), Marga Institute, WHO publication.

Hanna, S.S., C. Folke and K.G. Maler (Ed) 1996. *Rights to nature: Ecological, Economic, Cultural and Political Principles of Institutions for the Environment*, Covelo, California, USA: Island Press.

Harlan, J. 1995. *The living fields: Our agricultural heritage*, New York, USA: Cambridge University Press.

Haram, Liv. 1991. "Tswana Medicine in Interaction with Bio Medicine", *Social Science and Medicine*, Vol. 33, No. 2, pp. 167-175.

Hazra, Jayati. 2002. "Health and Development of North East India", *Geographical Review of India*, Vol. 64, No. 1, pp. 21-32.

Hunn, E. 1999. "The value of subsistence for the future of the world" in V.D. Nazarea (Ed) *Ethno ecology: Situated knowledge and located lives,* Tucson, Arizona, USA: Arizona University Press, pp. 23-36.

Helly, Jason and Kiran Cherla. 1999. *Medicinal Plant Sector in India: A Review,* New Delhi: Bookwell Publisher, pp.59.

Hufford, J. David. 1997. "Folk Medicine and Health Culture in Contemporary Society", *Complementary and Alternative Therapies in Primary Care,* Vol. 24, No. 4, December, pp.723-741.

IDRC. 1991. "A patent on life ownership of plant and animal research", Ottawa. International Development Research Centre.

IDRC Publication. 1994. "Traditional Health System and Public Policy", Workshop papers, Ottawa.

International Encyclopaedia of Social Sciences. 1978. Vol. XIV, pp.365

Islam, Anwar. 1994. "Understanding traditional health systems: A sociological perspective", *Workshop paper on Traditional Health System and Public Policy,* pp. 71-83.

IUCN ICTFIP. 1997. "Indigenous peoples and sustainability: Cases and Actions", *International Union for the Conservation of Nature and Natural Resources Inter-Commission Task Force on Indigenous Peoples (IUCN ICTFIP),* Netherlands, Utrecht: International Books.

Jamkhanthang, T. and Thangchinlian, G. (Unpublished). *Paite Customary Laws,* Churachandpur, Manipur, India.

Jeffery, Roger. 1982. "Policies towards Indigenous Healers in Independent India", *Social Science and Medicine,* Vol. 16, pp. 1835-1841.

Kakar, D.N. 1988. *Primary Health Care and Traditional Medical Practitioners,* New Delhi: Sterling Press.

Kala, C.P., Dhyani, P.P. and Sajwan, B.S. 2006. "Developing the medicinal plants sector in Northern India: Challenges and opportunities", *Journal of Ethnobiology and Ethnomedicine,* 2: 1-15.

Kamkhenthang, H. 1988. *The Paite: A Transborder Tribe of India and Burma,* Delhi: Mittal Publications.

Kamei, Gangmumei. 2000. 'Problem of Development in the Hill Areas of Manipur', in M. Horam (ed.), *The Rising Manipur*, New Delhi: Manas Publications, p. 68.

Kothari, Ashish and R. V. Anuradha. 1997. "Biodiversity, Intellectual Property Rights, and GATT Agreement: How to Address the Conflicts?" *Economic and Political Weekly*, Vol. 32, No. 43 (October 25-31,), pp. 2814-2820.

Krech, S. 1999. *The Ecological Indian: Myth and History*, New York, USA: W.W. Norton.

Koshy, Suresh. 1995. "The effect of TRIPS on Indian Patent Law: A Pharmaceutical Industry Perspective", *Boston University Journal of Science and Technology Law*, Vol.1, May.

Koul, A.K. and V.K Ahuja. 2001. *The Law of Intellectual Property Rights: In Prospect and Retrospect*, Faculty of Law, University of Delhi.

Kumar, Arun. 2002. "Globalization of the Indian Economy: Some Issues Pertaining to Public Health", *Workshop paper, organized by Centre for the study of Developing Societies and Centre of Social Medicine and Community Health*, 18th-20th January.

Kumar, Nagesh. 2003. "Intellectual Property Rights, Technology and Economic Development: Experiences of Asian Countries", *Economic and Political Weekly*, Vol. 38, No. 3 (January 18-24), pp. 209-215+217-226.

Lalitha, N. 2002. "Indian Pharmaceutical Industry in WTO Regime: A SWOT Analysis", *Economic and Political Weekly*, Vol. 37, No. 34 (August 24-30), pp. 3542-3555.

Lee, Rance P.L. 1982. "Comparative Studies of Health Care Systems", *Social Science and Medicine*, Vol. 16, pp. 629-642.

Lepage, P. 1994. "Indigenous peoples and the evolution of International standards: A short history" In M. Leger (Ed) *Aboriginal Peoples: Towards Self-government*, Montreal, Quebec, Canada, Black Rose Books, pp.1-24.

Liankhohau, T. 1993. *Social, Cultural, Economic and Religious Life of a Transformed Community (A Study of Paite Tribe)*, New Delhi: Gyan Publishing House.

McNeely, J.A. 1995. "The Impact of Human Activity on Biodiversity Assessment", *United Nations Environment Programme (UNEP)*, Cambridge University Press.

Mishra, D.N. 2001. "Evolution and development of Intellectual Property Rights" In Koul, A.K and Ahuja, V.K (Ed) *The Law of Intellectual Property Rights: In Prospect and Retrospect*, Faculty of Law, University of Delhi, pp. 49-51.

Michael P. Ryan. 1998. *Knowledge Diplomacy: Global Competition and the Politics of Intellectual Property*, Washington D.C, Brookings Institution Press, pp. 91-121.

Mudappa, Anjana and Sumy Oommen. 1998. "Need To Retread", *Amruth*, June, pp.10-13.

Mukhopadhya, Alok. 1992. "Indigenous Health Services—The State of the Art", State of India's Health, New Delhi: Voluntary Health Association of India.

Mukhopadhya, Alok (ed). 1997. "Report of the Independent Commission on Health in India" Voluntary Health Association of India, pp. 76-77.

Neumann, A.K. and P. Lauro. 1982. "Ethno-medicine and Bio-medicine Linking", *Social Science and Medicine*, Vol. 16, pp.1817-1824.

Nigh, Ronald. 2002. "Maya Medicine in the Biological Gaze Bio-prospecting Research as Herbal Fetishism", *Current Anthropology*, Vol. 43, No. 3, June, pp. 451-473.

Ostry, S. Aleck. 2001. "International Trade Regulation and Publicly Funded Health Care in Canada", *International Journal of Health Services*, Vol. 31, No. 3, pp. 475-480.

Palande, Dinkar D. 1987. "Alternative Systems of Medicine", *NAMAH (New Approach to Medicine and Health)*, pp.11-14.

Patni P.K. 2001. "Patent System in India" In Koul, A.K and Ahuja, V.K. (Ed) *The Law of Intellectual Property Rights: In Prospect and Retrospect*, Faculty of Law, University of Delhi, pp. 66-77.

Paul, B.D. 1955. *Health, Culture and Community*, New York: Russel Sage Foundation.

Pedersen, Duncan and Veronica Baruffati. 1989. "Healers, Deities, Saints and Doctors: Elements for the Analysis of Medical Systems", *Social Science and Medicine*, Vol. 29, No. 487-496.

Pillsbury, L.K. Barbara. 1982. "Policy and Evaluation Perspectives on Traditional Health Practitioners in National Health Care Systems", *Social Science and Medicine*, Vol. 16, pp. 1825-1835.

Posey, D.A. 1996. "Traditional Resource Rights: International Instruments for Protection and compensation for indigenous peoples and local communities", *International Union for the Conservation of Nature and Natural Resources, The World Conservation Union*, Gland, Switzerland.

Pushpangadan, P. 1989. "Research and Development in Tribal Medicine", In Buddhadeb Chaudhari and Dipankar Dasgupta (Eds) *Tribal Medicine*, pp. 321-324, Midnapore, Regional Research and Study Centre.

Qadeer, Imrana. 1985. "Health Services System in India: An expression of Socio-Economic Inequalities", *Social Action*, Vol. 35, July-September, pp.199-223.

Ramchandran, Prema. 2001. *Planning for Health—10th Plan Initiatives.*

Ramprasad, Vanaja. 1994. "Traditional Health Systems and Primary Health Care", *Workshop paper, IDRC*, pp.131-135.

Ramakrishnan, P.S. 1993. *'Shifting Agriculture and Sustainable Development: An interdisciplinary study from North Eastern India'*, pp. 424, Wiely Eastern, New Delhi, India.

RGI, 1991: *District census handbook of Churachandpur District*, Manipur, Census of India.

RGI, 2001. *Manipur, Series 14* (provisional population totals), Directorate of Census Operations Manipur, Census of India.

Sahai, Suman. 1996. "Importance of Indigenous Knowledge in IPR System", *Economic and Political Weekly*, Vol. 31, No. 47 (November. 23), pp. 3043-3045.

Sahai, Suman. 2001. "TRIPS Review: Basic Rights Must Be Restored", *Economic and Political Weekly*, Vol. 36, No. 31 (August 4-10), pp. 2918-2919.

Saraswati, B. (Ed.). 1991. *Tribal Thought and Culture*, pp. 13-24, Concept Publishing Company, New Delhi.

Schroff, Preeti and Shrawan Acharya. 2000. *Factors affecting utilization of Primary Health Care Centres in rural areas (a micro level study of PHC Por, Taluka Vadodara)*, School of Planning, Centre for Environmental Planning and Technology, Ahmedabad.

Segismundo, Ma Chona L. 1994. "Traditional Health Systems: Challenges in the Philippines", *Workshop Paper, IDRC*, pp.100-114.

Sen, Shipra. 1992. *Tribes and Castes of Manipur—Description and Bibliography*, Delhi: Mittal Publications.

Shankar, Darshan and S.N. Venugopal. 2000. "Malaria: The Indigenous understanding and management", *Amruth*, April, pp. 17-22.

Shanker Darshan. 1989. "Revitalization of Primary Health Care in Rural India : A Modern Challenge", In Buddhadeb Chaudhari and Dipankar Dasgupta (Eds) *Tribal Medicine*, pp. 241-245, Midnapore, Regional Research and Study Centre.

Shiva, Vandana. 1996. "Agricultural Biodiversity, Intellectual Property Rights and Farmers' Rights", *Economic and Political Weekly*, Vol. 31, No. 25 (June 22), pp. 1621-1623+1625-1631.

Shiva, Vandana. 1997. *Biopiracy: The Plunder of Nature and Knowledge*, South End Press, pp. 81, Cambridge (noting that TRIPS was conceived and shaped by coalitions of U.S., Japanese and European Corporations).

Shiva, Vandana. 2001. *Patents-Myths and Reality*, Penguin Books India.

Shiva, Vandana and Shalini Bhutani. 2001. An Activist Handbook on "Intellectual Property Rights and Patents", Research Foundation for Science, Technology and Ecology.

Shodhini. 1997. "Touch me, touch-me-not", Kali for Women.

Singh, Kavaljit. 2001. "Patents vs. Patients: AIDS, TNCs and Drug Price Wars", *Janata*, May 27, pp. 3-8.

Singh, N. Mohendro. 2002. *"Development Experience in Manipur"*, Imphal: Institute of Development Studies.

Sinha, Jai B.P., Hetukar Jha & Rajeshwar Mishra. 1999. "ASSERT searches for better health scenario (A summarized version of the report) 'the cultural context of health and healing' ", *The Social Engineer*, July, Vol. 8, No. 2, pp. 33-45.

Sindiga, I. 1995. *Traditional Medicine in Africa*, Nairobi, Kenya: East African Publishing House.

Singh, Ram. 2002. "Implementation of IPRs regime: The Justification Question", *Social Scientist*, Vol. 30, Nos. 1-2, January-February. 2002, pp. 61-82.

Soren, Gideon. 1997. *Report of the interview with tribal Medical Practitioners.* Semiliguda, WIDA (Mimeo).

Srinivasan, S. 1994. "Management of rural health care services in India: An overview", *Journal of Rural Development*, Vol. 13 (4), pp. 551-564.

Stork, N.E. 1999. "The magnitude of global biodiversity and its decline" In J. Cracraft and F.T. Grifo (Ed), *The living planet in crisis: biodiversity science and policy*, New York, USA: Columbia University Press, pp. 3-32.

Taylor, Carl E, Leslie Charles. 1973. "Asian Medical Systems: A Symposium on the role of comparative sociology in improving health care", *Social Science and Medicine*, Vol. 7, pp. 307-318.

Ved, D.K. 1997. "Trade in Medicinal plants—The State of our ignorance", *Amruth*, August, pp. 2-7.

Venne, S.H. 1998. *Our elders understand our rights: evolving international law regarding indigenous rights,* Penticon, British Columbia, Canada: Theytus Books Limited.

Voluntary Health Association of Manipur. 1995. Study on the Rural Health Services in Manipur (unpublished).

Warren, D. M., Slikkerveer L.J., and Brokensha D., (Ed). 1995. *The Cultural Dimension of Development: Indigenous Knowledge Systems,* London, UK: Intermediate Technology Publications.

Wayland, Coral. 2001. "Gendering Local Knowledge: Medicinal Plant Use and Primary Health Care in the Amazon", *Medical Anthropology Quarterly*, 15 (2): 171-188.

WHO South East Asia. 1992. *The Use of Traditional Medicine in Primary Health Care*, Delhi: All India Traveller Bookseller.

WHO. 1978. *Primary Health Care,* A joint report by the Director-General of the World Health Organization and the Executive Director of the United Nations Children's Fund, Geneva-New York.

World Trade Organization. 2000. "Protection of Biodiversity and Traditional Knowledge: The Indian Experience", *Committee on*

Trade and Environment Council for Trade-Related Aspects of Intellectual Property Rights, WT/CTE/W/156 IP/C/W/198, 14 July.

WRI & IIED. 1986. "World Resources", World Resources Institute and International Institute of Environment and Development, New York, Basis Books.

Young, David E. 1994. "Models of health care pluralism", *Workshop paper on Traditional Health System and Public Policy, IDRC*, pp. 62-70.

Zhang, Xiaorui. 1994. "WHO's Policy and Activities on Traditional Medicine", *Workshop paper, IDRC*, pp.139-142.

Index